# FEAST OF FLAVOURS
## from the Balinese Kitchen

# FEAST OF **FLAVOURS**

## from the *Balinese* Kitchen

### A STEP-BY-STEP CULINARY ADVENTURE

Heinz von Holzen

**Marshall Cavendish** Cuisine

Photographer: Heinz von Holzen

Published by Marshall Cavendish Editions
An imprint of Marshall Cavendish International
1 New Industrial Road, Singapore 536196

Other Marshall Cavendish Offices

Marshall Cavendish Ltd. 119 Wardour Street, London W1F OUW, UK • Marshall Cavendish Corporation. 99 White Plains Road, Tarrytown NY 10591-9001, USA • Marshall Cavendish Beijing. D31A, Huatingjiayuan, No. 6, Beisihuanzhonglu, Chaoyang District, Beijing, The People's Republic of China, 100029 • Marshall Cavendish International (Thailand) Co Ltd. 253 Asoke, 12th Flr, Sukhumvit 21 Road, Klongtoey Nua, Wattana, Bangkok 10110, Thailand • Marshall Cavendish (Malaysia) Sdn Bhd, Times Subang, Lot 46, Subang Hi-Tech Industrial Park, Batu Tiga, 40000 Shah Alam, Selangor Darul Ehsan, Malaysia

Marshall Cavendish is a trademark of Times Publishing Limited

**National Library Board Singapore Cataloguing in Publication Data**

Holzen, Heinz von.
Feast of flavours from the Balinese kitchen : a step-by-step culinary adventure / Heinz von Holzen. –
Singapore : Marshall Cavendish Cuisine, c2005.
p. cm. – (Feast of flavours)
Includes index.
ISBN : 981-232-676-6

1. Cookery, Balinese. I. Title. II. Series: Feast of flavours

TX724.5.I5
641.595986 – dc21            SLS2005034843

Printed in Singapore by Saik Wah Press Pte Ltd

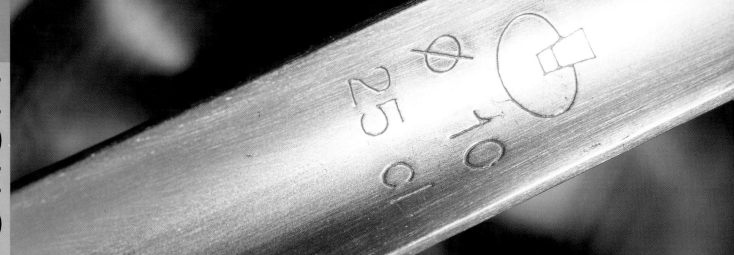

# COOKING TECHNIQUES

Balinese cooking techniques are very simple and vary little from those in other cultures and cuisines. The traditional source of heat was, and still is in many homes, a simple wood fire. In more modern homes, often a kerosene or gas stove makes life just a little easier. Cooking vessels are simple and mostly made from sheet iron and sometimes from aluminium. Very rarely and only for a few dishes, a wok finds its way to the stove. The Balinese also tend to use very low heat when cooking. This means that it is important to have plenty of time when preparing Balinese food.

## Blanching and Parboiling

Blanching is a basic cooking process frequently used for leafy vegetables such as water convolvulus, spinach or fern tips. Harder vegetables such as long beans and cabbage are parboiled, or lowered into boiling water for partial cooking or softening. To blanch vegetables, the ratio of water to vegetables must be ten to one (10:1). The water should be well salted and boiling rapidly before vegetables are added.

Blanching can also be used to cleanse bones meant for a stock. Place well washed bones in cold water and bring to a slow boil. This opens the pores and allows the impurities to flow out.

## Boiling and Simmering

When it comes to boiling or simmering, it is important to know whether the food item should begin in cold or hot liquid. Always add rice or noodles into rapidly boiling liquid, for instance, as this will prevent the rice or the noodles from sticking together, and stir frequently when boiling.

Meats such as chicken or beef should be added to simmering liquid or stock, which will close the pores and prevent the meat juices from being leached out and becoming dry. Do not cover the pot as this will intensify the heat, increase boiling motions and in the case of stocks, make them cloudy.

For dry beans (Green Bean Pudding; pg 102) or black glutinous rice (Black Rice Pudding; pg 96), start with cold liquid and bring to a quick boil, then reduce heat and simmer over low heat until done. Do not cover.

## Steaming

One of Bali's most used cooking methods, steaming is used daily for meat, fish, rice, vegetables, sausages and sweet snacks. Steaming is a gentle cooking process and food cooked in such a manner retains many nutrients and vitamins and, at the same time, maintains a most pleasant appearance.

To steam properly, first bring water in a steamer to a rapid boil, then position a steamer rack inside with items to be cooked on top. Lastly, cover with a heavy lid. The Balinese use a traditional steamer basket which also adds a certain flavour and aroma to the food steamed. Add some lemon grass, ginger and galangal to the boiling liquid for enhanced fragrance.

## Poaching

Poaching is suitable for such diverse food items as sausages, fish, eggs, dumplings and bananas. Heat liquid (water or stock) to 70–80°C / 158–176°F, then add in food to be poached. Never cover the pot. This is a gentle cooking process that retains the flavour, colour and shape of food.

Note: Covering the pot when poaching immediately increases heat and with that, the liquid would start to boil and cause many of the proteins, vitamins and minerals to be discharged and result in a loss of flavour, colour and shape.

## Deep-frying

Deep-frying is easily the most widely practised cooking method in Bali. This is because it only requires a vessel to cook in and plenty of oil. If not done properly, however, which is almost always the case in Bali, deep-frying becomes a most unhealthy and fattening way of cooking.

To deep-fry well, always use oil which is neutral in flavour and suitable for heating. Peanut, soy and corn oils are ideal. The ratio of oil to food should be ten to one (10:1). Never lower large quantities of food into the heated oil as this will rapidly cool down the oil, open the pores of the food being cooked and cause the food to absorb excess oil. Instead, heat oil to 160–180°C / 320–356°F, then add small quantities of food, which must be very dry, and fry at increasing heat. Drain cooked items thoroughly—first on a draining rack, then on paper towels.

## Stir-frying

This must be without any doubt Asia's most popular cooking method and yet it is seldom employed in Balinese cooking. Contrary to deep-frying, the food here is not cooked in the oil and then drained. In stir-frying, the oil becomes part of the dish. A good steel wok, relatively high heat and good quality oil form the foundation of a successful stir-fry. Unlike Chinese cooking, the heat source in Bali is mostly a wood fire and as such, the heat is relatively low. This means that the Balinese cook will be unable to whip up a quick stir-fry as it will take a lot longer to prepare a dish.

## Sautéing or Pan-frying

This is a very quick, basic cooking method for tender cuts. Heat oil in a shallow frying pan (skillet) to medium-high hotness, add fish fillets or meat, sear both sides and continue cooking until food is cooked through. Avoid having the heat reduce considerably as this will cause the pores of the meat or fish to open and lead to a loss of liquid or juices and toughen the food. For the same reason, always add salt only at the end. For vegetables, heat oil in a shallow pan to medium hotness, then add vegetables and sauté, stirring continuously.

## Grilling or Broiling

This very popular cooking method is mostly used for the preparation of saté, fish and food wrapped with banana leaves.

For saté and other tender cuts, which are always cooked over glowing charcoal, ensure that the fire is very low and the heat very high. This, in Bali, is achieved by vigorously fanning air into the fire, which is done by a sturdy, hand-held bamboo fan. The heat should be as high as possible so that the skewers of saté are lightly burnt, which will add the desired slightly bitter, smoky aftertaste.

For fish, start grilling first over very high heat, which will close the pores, then finish the grilling over lower heat. Avoid having meat juices drip into the fire as this will cause the flames to leap up and add a very unpleasant burnt flavour to the food.

Frequently baste grilled foods with an oil-based basting liquid to prevent the food and the spices from burning and, at the same time, to ensure that the flavours of the seasoning penetrate the meat.

Note: Combining 125 g (4$^{1}/_{2}$ oz / $^{1}/_{2}$ cup) of spice paste (see pg 8) and 125 ml (4 fl oz / $^{1}/_{2}$ cup) of oil makes a delicious marinade. Always use the chicken spice paste for chicken, seafood spice paste for fish, beef spice paste for beef and basic spice paste for pork, duck, lamb or game.

## Roasting

Roasting is usually done to cook suckling pigs, whole ducks or chickens. Traditionally, roasting in Bali is done over an open fire on a spit or when food is wrapped in various kinds of leaves, then buried under hot charcoal. In the modern kitchen, use a traditional oven. For the first 15–20 minutes, roast at high heat or 180–200°C / 350–400°F, then reduce the heat to 150–180°C / 300–350°F. Frequently baste food with an oil-based basting liquid.

## Braising or Glazing

This cooking method is more for secondary or tough cuts of meat, chicken and duck. Begin by heating oil in a heavy pan, then add meat and seal pores with frequent stirring until colour changes. Add all the spices and other ingredients, except liquid, and sauté again for a few minutes. Finally, add liquid and braise meat over low heat until done. Stewing is very much similar to braising, except that lower heat is used. Note the following points for a successful braised or stewed dish:

1. Always use a stew pan, which is wide and shallow, and not a pot.
2. Always use cheap, secondary cuts such as brisket, shoulder or neck. Avoid using tender cuts because they cook too quickly and do not allow the sauce to develop a rich, meaty flavour.
3. The ratio of meat to liquid should be two to one (2:1) when liquid is added the first time. Keep liquid as short as possible and top up with small amounts as liquid evaporates during the cooking process. This ensures that the sauce at the end will have the right, thickened consistency and the meat will have a shiny coating.
4. Never cover the pan when stewing.
5. Do not cook stews from start to finish in one go. Stew for about an hour or until meat is 75 per cent done, then remove from heat, leave to cool and refrigerate until the dish is required. Finally, reheat the stew and simmer until meat is tender, then season to taste and serve.

# BASIC RECIPES

## Basic Spice Paste (*Base Gede*)

**Ingredients**

| | |
|---|---|
| Red chillies | 300 g (10 oz), large, halved, seeded and sliced |
| Shallots | 500 g (1 lb 1<sup>1</sup>/2 oz), peeled and sliced |
| Garlic | 100 g (3<sup>1</sup>/2 oz), peeled and sliced |
| Ginger | 75 g (2<sup>1</sup>/2 oz), peeled and sliced |
| Galangal (*laos*) | 75 g (2<sup>1</sup>/2 oz), peeled and chopped |
| Lesser galangal (*kencur*) | 100 g (3<sup>1</sup>/2 oz), peeled and sliced |
| Turmeric | 175 g (6 oz), peeled and sliced |
| Candlenuts | 75 g (2<sup>1</sup>/2 oz) |
| Dried prawn (shrimp) paste (*terasi*) | 2 Tbsp, roasted |
| Coriander seeds | 2 Tbsp, crushed |
| Black peppercorns | 1 Tbsp, crushed |
| Freshly grated nutmeg | 1/4 tsp |
| Cloves | 8, crushed |
| Vegetable oil | 150 ml (5 fl oz) |
| **Lemon grass** | **2 stalks, bruised** |
| *Salam* **leaves** | **2** |
| **Salt** | **3/4 Tbsp** |
| **Water** | **250 ml (8 fl oz / 1 cup)** |

## Beef Spice Paste (*Base be Sampi*)

**Ingredients**

| | |
|---|---|
| Red chillies | 250 g (9 oz), large, halved, seeded and sliced |
| Bird's eye chillies | 40 g (1<sup>1</sup>/4 oz), finely sliced |
| Shallots | 200 g (7 oz), peeled and sliced |
| Garlic | 50 g (2 oz), peeled and sliced |
| Ginger | 50 g (2 oz), peeled and sliced |
| Galangal (*laos*) | 150 g (5 oz), peeled and chopped |
| Candlenuts | 100 g (3<sup>1</sup>/2 oz) |
| Coriander seeds | 2 Tbsp, crushed |
| Black peppercorns | 2 Tbsp, crushed |
| Palm sugar | 40 g (1<sup>1</sup>/4 oz), chopped |
| Vegetable oil | 150 ml (5 fl oz) |
| *Salam* **leaves** | **3** |
| **Salt** | **3/4 Tbsp** |
| **Water** | **250 ml (8 fl oz / 1 cup)** |

## Chicken Spice Paste (*Base be Siap*)

**Ingredients**

| | |
|---|---|
| Bird's eye chillies | 50 g (2 oz), finely sliced |
| Shallots | 225 g (7<sup>1</sup>/2 oz), peeled and sliced |
| Garlic | 125 g (4<sup>1</sup>/2 oz), peeled and sliced |
| Lesser galangal (*kencur*) | 50 g (2 oz), peeled and sliced |
| Turmeric | 125 g (4<sup>1</sup>/2 oz), peeled and sliced |
| Candlenuts | 100 g (3<sup>1</sup>/2 oz) |
| Palm sugar | 50 g (2 oz), chopped |
| Vegetable oil | 150 ml (5 fl oz) |
| **Lemon grass** | **2 stalks, bruised** |
| *Salam* **leaves** | **3** |
| **Salt** | **3/4 Tbsp** |
| **Water** | **250 ml (8 fl oz / 1 cup)** |

## Seafood Spice Paste (*Base be Pasih*)

**Ingredients**

| | |
|---|---|
| Red chillies | 450 g (16 oz / 1 lb), large, halved, seeded and sliced |
| Shallots | 225 g (7<sup>1</sup>/2 oz), peeled and sliced |
| Garlic | 50 g (2 oz), peeled and sliced |
| Ginger | 100 g (3<sup>1</sup>/2 oz), peeled and sliced |
| Turmeric | 175 g (6 oz), peeled and sliced |
| Candlenuts | 125 g (4<sup>1</sup>/2 oz) |
| Dried prawn (shrimp) paste (*terasi*) | 2 Tbsp, roasted |
| Coriander seeds | 2 Tbsp, crushed |
| Tomatoes | 200 g (7 oz), halved and seeded |
| Vegetable oil | 150 ml (5 fl oz) |
| **Tamarind pulp** | **2<sup>1</sup>/2 Tbsp** |
| **Lemon grass** | **2 stalks, bruised** |
| *Salam* **leaves** | **3** |
| **Salt** | **3/4 Tbsp** |
| **Water** | **250 ml (8 fl oz / 1 cup)** |

## Vegetable Spice Paste (*Base Jukut*)

**Ingredients**

| | |
|---|---|
| Red chillies | 250 g (9 oz), large, halved, seeded and sliced |
| Bird's eye chillies | 25 g (1 oz) |
| Shallots | 100 g (3<sup>1</sup>/2 oz), peeled and sliced |
| Garlic | 100 g (3<sup>1</sup>/2 oz), peeled and sliced |
| Galangal (*laos*) | 100 g (3<sup>1</sup>/2 oz), peeled and chopped |
| Lesser galangal (*kencur*) | 100 g (3<sup>1</sup>/2 oz), washed and sliced |
| Turmeric | 100 g (3<sup>1</sup>/2 oz), peeled and sliced |
| Candlenuts | 200 g (7 oz) |
| Dried prawn (shrimp) paste (*terasi*) | 1 Tbsp |
| Coriander seeds | 1 Tbsp, crushed |
| Black peppercorns | 1/2 Tbsp, crushed |
| Vegetable oil | 150 ml (5 fl oz) |
| *Salam* **leaves** | **2** |
| **Lemon grass** | **2 stalks, bruised** |
| **Water** | **250 ml (8 fl oz / 1 cup)** |
| **Salt** | **3/4 Tbsp** |

## Method

- For each spice paste recipe, combine all ingredients except those in bold using a mortar and pestle, blender (processor) or ideally, a meat grinder fitted with a medium blade; grind coarsely.
- Transfer paste to a heavy saucepan. Add remaining ingredients and simmer over medium heat for about 1 hour or until water has evaporated and paste becomes golden in colour.
- Leave to cool thoroughly before using or storing for future use; one way is to portion into ice cube trays and freeze.

**Note:** Use chicken spice paste for chicken, beef spice paste for beef or basic spice paste for pork, duck, lamb or game.

# Spiced Tomato Sauce (Sambel Tomat)

### Ingredients

| | |
|---|---|
| Vegetable oil | 150 ml (5 fl oz) |
| Shallots | 200 g (7 oz), peeled and sliced |
| Garlic | 100 g (3 1/2 oz), peeled and sliced |
| Red chillies | 375 g (12 1/2 oz), large, seeded and sliced |
| Bird's eye chillies | 375 g (12 1/2 oz), left whole |
| Palm sugar | 50 g (2 oz), chopped |
| Dried prawn (shrimp) paste (terasi) | 1 1/2 Tbsp, roasted |
| Tomatoes | 750 g (1 lb 10 oz), peeled and seeded |
| Lime juice | 1 Tbsp |
| Salt | to taste |

### Method

- Heat oil in a heavy saucepan over moderate high heat. Add shallots and garlic and sauté until golden.
- Add chillies and sauté until chillies are soft, then add palm sugar and prawn paste. Sauté until sugar caramelises.
- Add tomatoes and sauté until tomatoes are soft. Remove from heat and leave to cool. Add small amounts of water if dry.
- Coarsely grind cooled ingredients using a mortar and pestle or a blender (processor).
- Adjust sauce to taste with lime juice and salt before serving.

# Shallot and Lemon Grass Dressing (Sambel Matah)

### Ingredients

| | |
|---|---|
| Shallots | 40 g (1 1/4 oz), peeled, halved and finely sliced |
| Lemon grass | 75 g (2 1/2 oz), bruised, finely sliced and chopped |
| Garlic | 20 g (3/4 oz), peeled and finely chopped |
| Bird's eye chillies | 30 g (1 oz), finely sliced |
| Kaffir lime leaves | 2, finely chopped |
| Dried prawn (shrimp) paste (terasi) | 1/2 tsp, roasted and finely crumbled |
| Lime juice | 2 Tbsp, freshly squeezed |
| Vegetable oil | 4 Tbsp |
| Salt | a pinch |
| Ground black pepper | a pinch |

### Method

- Combine all ingredients except salt and pepper in a large bowl. Mix thoroughly for 5 minutes. Season to taste with salt and pepper before using.
- Alternatively, heat oil in a saucepan and cook all ingredients over medium heat for 5 minutes or until fragrant. Remove from heat and leave to cool to room temperature before using.

## Stock (*Kuah*)

### Ingredients

| | |
|---|---|
| Chicken, beef, pork or duck bones | 5 kg (11 lb), skin and fat discarded, then chopped into 2.5-cm (1-inch) pieces |
| Spice paste | 375 g (12$^1$/$_2$ oz), according to type of bones used (see note on pg 9) |
| Lemon grass | 1 stalk, bruised |
| Kaffir lime leaves | 3, torn |
| Red chillies | 2, bruised |
| Bird's eye chillies | 3 |
| *Salam* leaves | 2 |
| Black peppercorns | 1 Tbsp, coarsely crushed |
| Coriander seeds | 1 Tbsp, crushed |

### Method

- Rinse bones until water is clear. Place into a stockpot and add sufficient cold water to cover. Bring to the boil over high heat.
- Drain bones and discard liquid. Rinse bones again, then place into a larger stockpot. Add 3 times as much water as there are bones. Bring to the boil, reduce heat and skim off scum.
- Add remaining ingredients and simmer stock over very low heat for 5–6 hours. If making pork stock, simmer for 2 hours.

**Note:** A carefully prepared basic stock is essential to any quality soup or sauce. Stocks must always be cooked slowly and uncovered. Covering the pot will increase the heat and cause the stock to boil, which makes the stock cloudy. Scum and fat also should be removed as they surface. When preparing any stock, never add salt at the beginning because it makes the resulting stock salty. If you wish to freeze the stock for future use, first reduce it to a syrupy consistency over medium heat, then leave it to cool to room temperature before pouring into ice cube trays to freeze.

## Vegetable Stock (*Kuah Sayur*)

### Ingredients

| | |
|---|---|
| Vegetable oil | 2 Tbsp |
| Shallots | 75 g (2$^1$/$_2$ oz), peeled and sliced |
| Garlic | 50 g (2 oz), peeled and sliced |
| Vegetable spice paste (see pg 8) | 125 g (4$^1$/$_2$ oz) |
| Leek | 75 g (2$^1$/$_2$ oz), sliced |
| Celery | 75 g (2$^1$/$_2$ oz), sliced, including stems and leaves |
| Cabbage | 75 g (2$^1$/$_2$ oz), sliced |
| Spring onions (scallions) | 100 g (3$^1$/$_2$ oz), sliced |
| Tomatoes | 300 g (10 oz), diced |
| Water | 2 litres (8 cups / 3$^1$/$_5$ pints) |
| Bird's eye chillies | 2, bruised |
| Lemon grass | 2 stalks, bruised |
| Kaffir lime leaves | 2, torn |
| Coriander seeds | 1 tsp, crushed |
| Black peppercorns | $^1$/$_2$ tsp, crushed |

### Method

- Heat oil in heavy saucepan. Add shallots and garlic and sauté until fragrant.
- Add spice paste and sauté again until shallots and garlic are evenly coated and paste is fragrant.
- Add leek, celery, cabbage, spring onions and tomatoes. Sauté over medium high heat until vegetables are soft.
- Pour in water and add all remaining ingredients. Bring to the boil and simmer for 2 hours over medium heat.
- Strain stock using cloth or a sieve. Press on vegetables to release as much liquid and flavour as possible.

**Note:** For the best possible flavour, use very ripe vegetables, herbs and spices when preparing stock.

# COOKING UTENSILS

### Mortar and Pestle or Stone Grinder

By far the most important utensil, this is used for grinding, crushing and making spice pastes so central to the flavours of Bali. Choose a mortar that is slightly curved, heavy, sturdy and roughly textured. If available, purchase a mortar and pestle carved from volcanic rock because it is harder and, hence, more durable. This is because many spices are hard and require considerable force to grind by hand.

### Food Processor or Meat Grinder

Most spice mixtures can be ground or better chopped in one of these kitchen aids, which are today a common sight even in Bali. Especially during ceremonies, when meals for the whole village are prepared, the villagers often replace the heavy stone mortar sitting on the ground with a meat grinder. If using a blender (food processor), the ingredients should be roughly chopped first and a little oil and water should be added while blending.

### Pots and Pans

It is worthwhile to invest in good quality stainless steel or even copper pans. These materials will withstand years of reasonable usage, as well as remain hygenic and resistant to the corrosive action of certain foods and cleaning agents. They also will not impart an odour, colour or taste to the food. Stainless steel or copper pans distribute heat much more evenly and are less prone to hot spots, which cause food to stick and burn.

Several pots and pans, consisting of a basic range, are recommended. They are a 10–15-litre (2$^1$/$_2$–4 gallon) stockpot; a stew pan (*above*); a shallow sauté or frying pan (skillet); a medium-sized pot; and finally, a perforated insert which can be placed inside the pot so that food can be steamed.

### Wok

Contrary to Western beliefs, woks are rather seldom used in a Balinese kitchen. Nevertheless, a heavy steel wok with a diameter of 30–35 cm (12–14-inches) is ideal for home use.

### Rice Cooker

Because of the amount of rice Balinese people eat and the number of people cooked for, many households now use an electric rice cooker. A heavy saucepan with a perforated insert and a tight-fitting lid will work just as well.

### Knives

As is the case with Western cooks, the Balinese use a variety of knives for various tasks. As a lot of food such as meats, fish and spices require chopping, there is always a heavy chopping knife on hand. Smaller knives are used to clean, cut, trim or slice vegetables, fruits, meats or spices.

### Cutting Board or Chopping Block

Often meats or fish used in Balinese cooking can be rather tough or very dry which is why they are often minced. To do so easily, a heavy chopping board is most useful. It is a good idea for safety and sanitation reasons not to use one board for all tasks. Instead, have several differently coloured boards in the kitchen, for fish, meat, vegetables and fruit.

### Grater and Shredder

A high quality stainless steel grater or shredder is useful for the grating of vegetables, coconuts, nutmeg or lime zest.

### Measuring Spoons, Ladles and Scales

All recipes in this book are based on metric measures and it is recommended that the recipes are followed accurately. As such, it ideal to get an electronic scale with a range from 1 g to 2 kg ($^1/_{30}$ oz to 4 lb 6 oz) and a set of stainless steel measuring spoons and ladles. It is absolutely essential that all basic recipes, such as the spice pastes and spiced tomato sauce, are followed faithfully for the consistent outcome of dishes.

# Weights & Measures

Quantities for this book are given in Metric and American (spoon and cup) measures. Standard spoon and cup measurements used are: 1 teaspoon = 5 ml, 1 dessertspoon = 10 ml, 1 tablespoon = 15 ml, 1 cup = 250 ml. All measures are level unless otherwise stated.

## LIQUID AND VOLUME MEASURES

| Metric | Imperial | American |
|---|---|---|
| 5 ml | $\frac{1}{6}$ fl oz | 1 teaspoon |
| 10 ml | $\frac{1}{3}$ fl oz | 1 dessertspoon |
| 15 ml | $\frac{1}{2}$ fl oz | 1 tablespoon |
| 60 ml | 2 fl oz | $\frac{1}{4}$ cup (4 tablespoons) |
| 85 ml | $2\frac{1}{2}$ fl oz | $\frac{1}{3}$ cup |
| 90 ml | 3 fl oz | $\frac{3}{8}$ cup (6 tablespoons) |
| 125 ml | 4 fl oz | $\frac{1}{2}$ cup |
| 180 ml | 6 fl oz | $\frac{3}{4}$ cup |
| 250 ml | 8 fl oz | 1 cup |
| 300 ml | 10 fl oz ($\frac{1}{2}$ pint) | $1\frac{1}{4}$ cup |
| 375 ml | 12 fl oz | $1\frac{1}{2}$ cup |
| 435 ml | 14 fl oz | $1\frac{3}{4}$ cup |
| 500 ml | 16 fl oz | 2 cups |
| 625 ml | 20 fl oz (1 pint) | $2\frac{1}{2}$ cups |
| 750 ml | 24 fl oz ($1\frac{1}{5}$ pint) | 3 cups |
| 1 litre | 32 fl oz ($1\frac{3}{5}$ pint) | 4 cups |
| 1.25 litres | 40 fl oz (2 pints) | 5 cups |
| 1.5 litres | 48 fl oz ($2\frac{2}{5}$ pints) | 6 cups |
| 2.5 litres | 80 fl oz (4 pints) | 10 cups |

## OVEN TEMPERATURE

| Regulo | °C | °F | Gas |
|---|---|---|---|
| Very slow | 120 | 250 | 1 |
| Slow | 150 | 300 | 2 |
| Moderately slow | 160 | 325 | 3 |
| Moderate | 180 | 350 | 4 |
| Moderately hot | 190/200 | 370/400 | 5/6 |
| Hot | 210/220 | 410/440 | 6/7 |
| Very hot | 230 | 450 | 8 |
| Super hot | 250/290 | 475/550 | 9/10 |

## ABBREVIATION

| | |
|---|---|
| Tbsp | tablespoon |
| tsp | teaspoon |
| kg | kilogram |
| g | gram |
| l | litres |
| ml | millilitres |

## DRY MEASURES

| Metric | Imperial |
|---|---|
| 30 g | 1 oz |
| 45 g | $1\frac{1}{2}$ oz |
| 55 g | 2 oz |
| 70 g | $2\frac{1}{2}$ oz |
| 85 g | 3 oz |
| 100 g | $3\frac{1}{2}$ oz |
| 110 g | 4 oz |
| 125 g | $4\frac{1}{2}$ oz |
| 140 g | 5 oz |
| 280 g | 10 oz |
| 450 g | 16 oz (1 lb) |
| 500 g | 1 lb, $1\frac{1}{2}$ oz |
| 700 g | $1\frac{1}{2}$ lb |
| 800 g | $1\frac{3}{4}$ lb |
| 1 kg | 2 lb, 3 oz |
| 1.5 kg | 3 lb, $4\frac{1}{2}$ oz |
| 2 kg | 4 lb, 6 oz |

## LENGTH

| Metric | Imperial |
|---|---|
| 0.5 cm | $\frac{1}{4}$ in |
| 1 cm | $\frac{1}{2}$ in |
| 1.5 cm | $\frac{3}{4}$ in |
| 2.5 cm | 1 in |

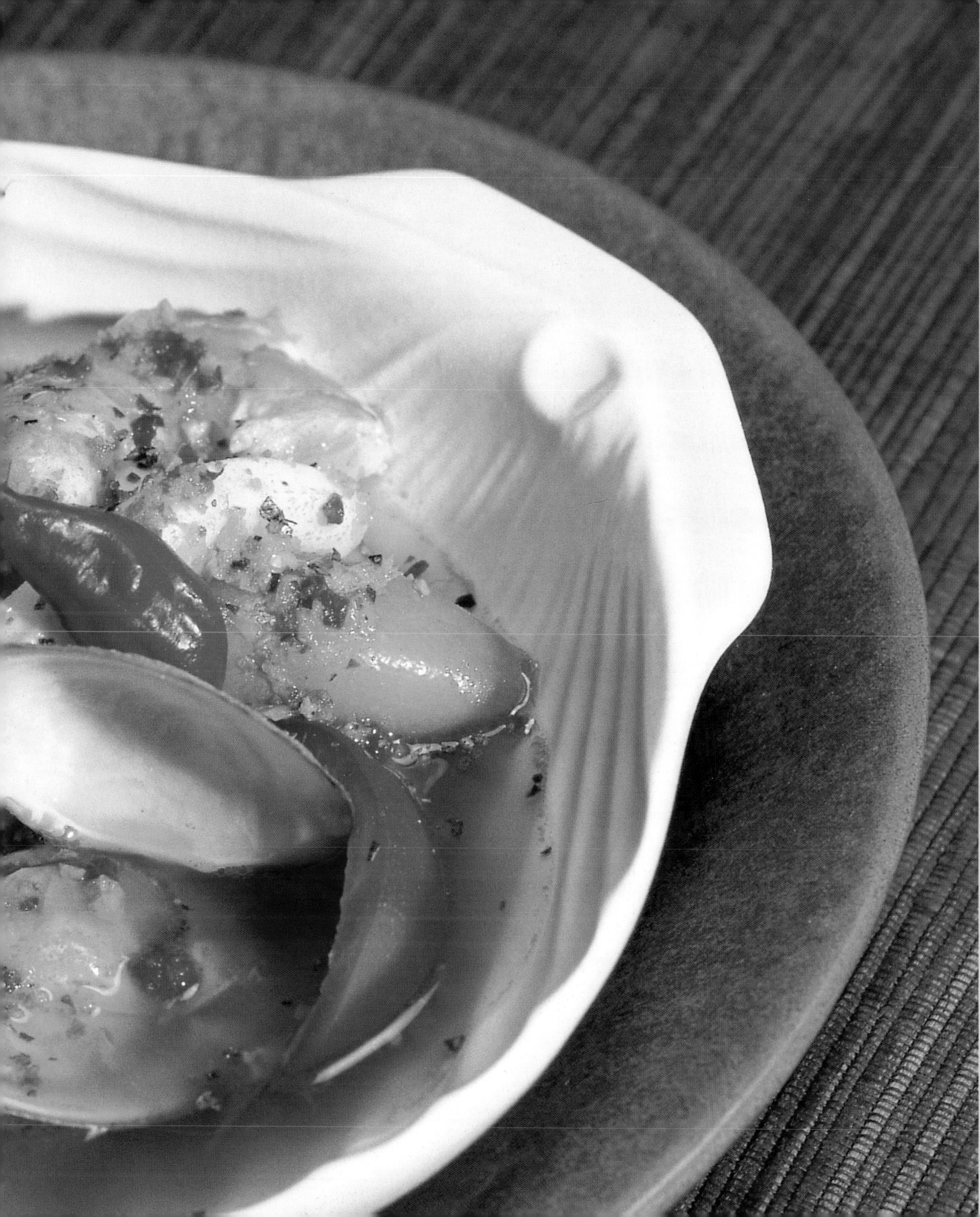

# SOUPS

For easier handling, halve papaya across and peel. After which, halve lengthways and deseed, then cut into 4–6 pieces lengthways. Slice across lengths for dice.

Sauté papaya until it changes colour before adding stock.

It is important that soup never reaches the boil after coconut milk is added. Boiling coconut milk draws out oil.

# GREEN PAPAYA SOUP
## (*GEDANG MEKUAH*)

Aromatic and deliciously creamy, this soup is suitable for vegetarians but not vegans because of the dried prawn paste in the vegetable spice paste.

### Ingredients

| | |
|---|---|
| Green papaya | 1, unripe, about 750 g (1 lb 10 oz) |
| Vegetable oil | 1 Tbsp |
| Vegetable spice paste (see pg 8) | 250 g (9 oz) |
| Lemon grass | 1 stalk, bruised |
| *Salam* leaves | 2 |
| Vegetable stock (see pg 10) | 1 litre (1³/₅ pints / 4 cups), or chicken stock |
| Coconut milk | 250 ml (8 fl oz / 1 cup) |
| Salt | a pinch or to taste |
| Crushed black peppercorns | a pinch or to taste |

### Garnish
Crisp-fried shallots
Chopped kaffir lime leaves

## Method

- Peel and deseed papaya, then cut into dice about 0.5-cm (¹/₂-inch) thick.
- Heat oil in a heavy soup pot. Add spice paste, lemon grass and *salam* leaves. Sauté until fragrant.
- Add papaya and continue to sauté until papaya is evenly coated with spice paste and changes colour.
- Pour in stock and mix well. Bring to the boil and simmer until papaya is 75 per cent cooked.

- Add coconut milk and simmer until papaya is tender. If liquid reduces too much, add more stock. Season to taste with salt and pepper.
- Garnish and serve.
- For variation, replace vegetable spice paste with that for seafood and garnish with diced, cooked seafood of choice.

# MUSHROOM SOUP
## (WONG DADAH)

With some steamed rice, this creamy and flavourful soup becomes a hearty meal.

### Ingredients

| | |
|---|---|
| Vegetable oil | 2 Tbsp |
| Vegetable spice paste (see pg 8) | 200 g (7 oz) |
| Shiitake mushrooms | 250 g (9 oz), washed and sliced or quartered |
| Chicken stock (see pg 10) | 625 ml (20 fl oz / 2¹/₂ cups) |
| Lemon grass | 1 stalk, bruised |
| Kaffir lime leaves | 2, bruised |
| Coconut cream | 250 ml (8 fl oz / 1 cup) |
| Salt | a pinch |
| Ground black pepper | a pinch |
| Crisp-fried shallots (optional) | 2 Tbsp |

Step-By-Step

The spice paste must be fragrant before mushrooms are added so that the resulting soup will be at its most flavourful.

After adding stock, lemon grass and lime leaves, bring to the boil over low heat. The slower, gentle cooking process gives the soup a better taste.

Similarly, after adding coconut cream, return to the boil over low heat.

### Method

- Heat oil in heavy saucepan. Add spice paste and sauté until fragrant.
- Add mushrooms and sauté for 2 minutes more.
- Add stock, lemon grass and lime leaves. Bring to the boil over low heat and simmer for 5 minutes.
- Add coconut cream. Return to the boil and simmer for 5 minutes.
- Season to taste with salt and pepper. Serve garnished with crisp-fried shallots, if using.

# BALINESE SEAFOOD SOUP
## (SOP IKAN)

The mixed seafood imparts a certain sweetness to this light and refreshing soup, while the blimbing adds hints of tartness and zest.

### Ingredients

| | |
|---|---|
| Prawns (shrimps) | 400 g (13½ oz), cleaned and deveined |
| Fish fillets | 8, cut into 50-g (2-oz) pieces |
| Clams or mussels | 4 |
| Salt | a pinch or to taste |
| Ground black pepper | a pinch or to taste |
| Seafood spice paste (see pg 8) | 4 Tbsp |
| Lime juice | 2 Tbsp |
| Vegetable oil | 1–2 Tbsp |
| Seafood, clam or chicken stock (see pg 10) | 1 litre (1³⁄₅ pints / 4 cups) |
| Salam leaves | 3 |
| Kaffir lime leaves | 2 |
| Blimbing | 2 |
| Tomatoes | 4, peeled, seeded and cut into wedges |

**Step-By-Step**

Properly wash and clean all ingredients, especially shellfish, to remove all traces of grit.

Mix seafood with spice paste and lime juice until well coated.

Cook seafood over very low heat to prevent overcooking, which toughens the meat, and retain their sweet juices.

### Method
- Season seafood with salt and pepper, then add spice paste and lime juice. Mix well.
- Heat oil in a heavy saucepan. Add seafood and sauté quickly until colour changes on both sides of prawns and fish.
- Add stock, salam and lime leaves and blimbing. Bring to the boil, then braise over very low heat until seafood is almost cooked and mussels open.
- Add tomato wedges and simmer until seafood is tender and tomatoes warmed through.
- Season to taste with salt and pepper. Serve.

Add chicken to stock only after it has been simmering for about 4 hours.

After shredding chicken meat, prepare other ingredients for use and set aside.

Add transparent noodles last, then return to the boil and season with salt before serving.

S
t
e
p
-
B
y
-
S
t
e
p

# CHICKEN SOUP WITH VEGETABLES AND EGGS
## (JUKUT SIAP)

With noodles, assorted vegetables and eggs added, this chicken soup makes a hearty meal.

### Ingredients

| | |
|---|---|
| Chicken stock (see pg 10) | 3 litres (4⁴/₅ pints / 12 cups) |
| Chicken | 1, about 1.2–1.5 kg (2 lb 10 oz–3 lb 4¹/₂ oz) |
| Chicken spice paste (see pg 8) | 2 Tbsp |
| Kaffir lime leaves | 2, torn |
| *Salam* leaves | 2 |
| Red chillies | 2, large, bruised |
| Bird's eye chillies | 2, bruised |
| Crushed black peppercorns | a pinch |
| Cabbage | 200 g (7 oz), finely shredded |
| Bean sprouts | 200 g (7 oz), cleaned |
| Chinese celery leaves | 50 g (2 oz), finely sliced |
| Spring onions (scallions) | 50 g (2 oz), finely sliced |
| Transparent (glass) noodles | 100 g (3¹/₂ oz), blanched to soften, then cooled in iced water |
| Salt | to taste |
| Hard-boiled eggs | 4, shelled and cut into wedges |
| Crisp-fried shallots | |

### Method

- Prepare chicken stock. When stock has simmered for 4 hours, add chicken. Simmer until chicken is very tender and meat almost falls off the bone, about 1 hour.
- Remove chicken from stock and place into a deep container. Strain chicken stock over chicken. Leave chicken to cool in stock.

- Drain chicken from cold stock. Separate meat from bones and shred very finely. Discard bones.
- Return stock to the boil. Add spice paste, lime and *salam* leaves, chillies and pepper. Simmer until liquid is reduced to about 1.5 litres (2²/₅ pints / 6 cups).
- Add cabbage, bean sprouts, celery and spring onions. Simmer for 2 minutes.

- Add shredded chicken and transparent noodles. Return to the boil and simmer for 2 minutes. Season to taste with salt.
- To serve, ladle soup into individual bowls and garnish with eggs and crisp-fried shallots.

Pickled Vegetables (*Acar*)

Corn and Fern Tips with Grated Coconut (*Jukut Urab*)

Steamed Mushrooms in Banana Leaf (*Pesan Wong*)

Fermented Soy Bean Cake in Sweet Soy Sauce (*Sambel Goreng Tempe*)

Mixed Vegetable Salad in Peanut Dressing (*Pecelan*)

Creamy Long Bean Salad (*Jukut Antungan*)

Vegetable and Prawn Salad (*Lawar Udang*)

Minced Duck and Green Papaya Salad (*Lawar Kwir*)

Jackfruit and Pork Salad (*Lawar Nangka*)

To prepare cucumbers for use, first cut off both ends of each cucumber, then halve lengthways. Remove pulpy core with a spoon before slicing across.

To prepare dressing, combine water, sugar, vinegar, ginger, lemon grass and salt in a pot. Bring to the boil and simmer for 1 minute.

Dressing has to be completely cooled before it is mixed with the cucumbers, shallots and chillies or it will cause them to wilt.

Step-By-Step

# PICKLED VEGETABLES
## (*ACAR*)

Serving this dish of pickled vegetables requires some planning ahead, but it rewards by refreshing the tongue with zesty, mildly spicy cucumber slices.

### *Ingredients*

| | |
|---|---|
| Water | 250 ml (8 fl oz / 1 cup) |
| Sugar | 250 g (9 oz) |
| Rice vinegar | 250 ml (8 fl oz / 1 cup), or white vinegar |
| Ginger | 50 g (2 oz), peeled and sliced |
| Lemon grass | 1 stalk or more to taste, bruised and tied into a knot |
| Salt | a pinch |
| Cucumbers | 3, medium, halved lengthways, cored and sliced |
| Shallots | 10, peeled and quartered |
| Bird's eye chillies | 10 |

### *Method*

- Combine water, sugar, vinegar, ginger, lemon grass and salt in a saucepan. Bring to the boil and simmer for 1 minute.
- Remove from heat and leave to cool thoroughly.
- Combine remaining ingredients and mix well with cooled dressing.
- Refrigerate for 24 hours before serving at room temperature.

# CORN AND FERN TIPS WITH GRATED COCONUT
## (JUKUT URAB)

Kaffir lime leaves, palm sugar and lesser galangal make the dressing for this crunchy salad delightfully bold and flavoursome.

### Ingredients

| | |
|---|---|
| Corn kernels | 300 g (10 oz), blanched |
| Fern tips | 300 g (10 oz), blanched |
| Red chillies (optional) | 2, large, seeded and sliced |
| Grated coconut | 250 g (9 oz), lightly roasted |
| Crisp-fried shallots | 3 Tbsp |

### Fried Chilli Dressing

| | |
|---|---|
| Vegetable oil | 4 Tbsp |
| Shallots | 100 g (3 1/2 oz), peeled and finely sliced |
| Garlic | 75 g (2 1/2 oz) |
| Bird's eye chillies | 25 g (3/4 oz), finely sliced |
| Dried prawn (shrimp) paste (terasi) | 1/2 tsp, roasted and finely crumbled |
| Salt | a pinch |

### Dressing (combined)

| | |
|---|---|
| Cooking oil | 2 Tbsp |
| Fried chilli dressing (sambal sereh tabia) | 4 Tbsp, see recipe |
| Kaffir lime leaves | 3, finely chopped |
| Salt | a pinch |
| Crushed black peppercorns | a pinch |
| Palm sugar | 1 Tbsp, chopped |
| Lesser galangal (kencur) | 40 g (1 1/4 oz), washed and finely ground |

Prepare crisp-fried shallots first, then set aside to cool and use as garnish later. This is because dressed salad cannot wait.

Prepare all salad ingredients next and set aside. To blanch vegetables, use the ratio of 1 part vegetables to 10 parts heavily salted, rapidly boiling water.

Add dressing to vegetables and toss only just before serving.

- Combine corn, fern tips, chillies and coconut in a large bowl. Mix well.
- Prepare fried chilli dressing. Heat oil in a frying pan (skillet).
- Add shallots and garlic and sauté for 2 minutes.
- Add chillies and dried prawn paste and continue to sauté until golden, then season with salt.
- Remove from heat and leave to cool before use.
- When ready to serve, add combined dressing ingredients to mixed vegetables and toss to mix.
- Garnish with crisp-fried shallots and serve immediately.

# STEAMED MUSHROOMS IN BANANA LEAF
## (PESAN WONG)

Nutritious, tasty and easy to prepare, the mushrooms here are tender, flavourful and mildly spicy.

### Ingredients

| | |
|---|---|
| Shiitake mushrooms | 250 g (9 oz), cleaned |
| Vegetable oil | 2 Tbsp |
| Vegetable spice paste (see pg 8) | 125 g (4¹/₂ oz) |
| Bird's eye chillies | 2, sliced |
| Dried prawn (shrimp) paste (*terasi*) | 1 tsp, roasted |
| Salt | a pinch |
| Banana leaves | 8, each 18 x 15 cm (7 x 6 inches) |
| Bamboo skewers or cocktail sticks | |

Spoon a hearty amount of seasoned mushrooms for 1 serving onto the centre of a banana leaf rectangle.

Fold in long edges of banana leaf to enclose the filling.

Secure both ends as shown with bamboo skewers or cocktail sticks.

### Method

- Dice cleaned mushrooms and set aside. If shiitake mushrooms are unavailable, use other types such as oyster, button, enokitake and nameko mushrooms or white and black fungus.
- Combine oil, spice paste, chillies, dried prawn paste and salt in a stone mortar. Grind to a fine paste.

- Transfer paste to a bowl, then mix in mushrooms.
- Place a generous portion of mushrooms onto the centre of a banana leaf.
- Fold banana leaf in thirds lengthways, then secure open ends with bamboo skewers or cocktail sticks.

- Steam parcels over moderate heat for 7–10 minutes. Parcels can be grilled for variation.
- If banana leaves are unavailable, replace with corn husks or vine leaves, which are preferable to greaseproof paper or aluminium foil.

Slice fermented soy bean cake into similarly sized pieces, about 5 x 1 cm (2 x 1/2 inch).

Heat oil for deep-frying until medium-hot, which is about 170°C/340°F, then add in fermented soy bean cake strips to cook.

Adding sweet soy sauce to the dish gives it not only a great flavour, but also a rich appetising colour.

# FERMENTED SOY BEAN CAKE IN SWEET SOY SAUCE
## (SAMBEL GORENG TEMPE)

Fermented soy bean cakes, or *tempe* (TEHM-peh) to the Indonesians, gain a distinctive nutty flavour when fried and are well complemented by the sweet soy sauce.

### Ingredients

| | |
|---|---|
| Fermented soy bean cake (tempe) | 400 g (13 1/2 oz) |
| Cooking oil for deep-frying | |
| Vegetable oil | 2 Tbsp |
| Shallots | 60 g (2 oz), peeled and sliced |
| Garlic | 40 g (1 1/4 oz), peeled and sliced |
| Red chillies | 40 g (1 1/4 oz), large, seeded and finely sliced |
| Galangal (laos) | 30 g (1 oz), peeled and sliced |
| Palm sugar | 20 g (3/4 oz), chopped |
| Sweet soy sauce (kecap manis) | 3 Tbsp |
| Vegetable stock (see pg 10) | 3 Tbsp |
| Tomato | 1, peeled, seeded and cut into strips |
| Salt | a pinch |
| Bird's eye chillies (optional) | 4, chopped |

### Method

- Slice fermented soy bean cake into similarly sized strips.
- Heat sufficient oil for deep-frying until medium-hot. Lower in soy bean cake pieces and fry until golden and crisp. Drain on absorbent paper towels.

- Heat 2 Tbsp oil in a frying pan (skillet). Add shallots, garlic, chillies and galangal. Sauté for 2–4 minutes.
- Add palm sugar and sweet soy sauce. Continue to sauté until evenly glazed.
- Add stock and when it boils, add tomato and sauté for 1 minute.

- Add fried soy bean cake and stir frequently until sauce has reduced and caramelised.
- Season to taste with salt and stir in bird's eye chillies, if using, just before serving.

Beginning with long beans, separately blanch all vegetables in rapidly boiling, salted water.

Plunge drained vegetables into ice water to stop the cooking process. Vegetables will remain crisp as a result.

Combine blanched vegetables in a large bowl and set aside. Mix in peanut sauce only just before serving.

Step-By-Step

# MIXED VEGETABLE SALAD IN PEANUT DRESSING
## (*PECELAN*)

This is the Balinese version of the famed Indonesian dish—Gado-Gado. In the Balinese version, water is used instead of coconut milk and the peanut sauce is only ground and not cooked.

### Ingredients

| | |
|---|---|
| Long (snake) beans | 100 g ($3^{1}/_{2}$ oz), cut into 4-cm (2-inch) lengths |
| Bean sprouts | 100 g ($3^{1}/_{2}$ oz) |
| Spinach | 100 g ($3^{1}/_{2}$ oz) |
| Cabbage | 100 g ($3^{1}/_{2}$ oz), thinly sliced |
| Salt | a pinch or to taste |
| Ground black pepper | a pinch or to taste |
| Crisp-fried shallots | 2 Tbsp |
| Shelled peanuts (groundnuts) | 2 Tbsp, can be dry-fried, fried in oil or oven-roasted, then crushed |
| Sweet soy sauce (*kecap manis*) | to taste |

### Peanut Sauce

| | |
|---|---|
| Peanuts (groundnuts) | 250 g (9 oz), skins left on and deep-fried until lightly brown |
| Garlic | 3 cloves, peeled and sliced |
| Bird's eye chillies | 1–3, finely sliced |
| Lesser galangal (*kencur*) | 25 g (1 oz), finely sliced |
| Sweet soy sauce (*kecap manis*) | 2 Tbsp |
| Palm sugar | 20 g ($^{3}/_{4}$ oz), chopped |
| Water | 250 ml (8 fl oz / 1 cup) |
| Salt | a pinch |

### Method

- Blanch all vegetables and plunge into ice water to cool. Drain well.
- Prepare peanut sauce. Combine all ingredients in a stone mortar and grind until very fine. Alternatively, combine in a blender (processor).
- Combine all vegetables in a large bowl and mix in peanut sauce. Season to taste with salt and pepper.
- Serve garnished with crisp-fried shallots, crushed peanuts and sweet soy sauce.
- If desired, serve salad with crispy, deep-fried fermented soy bean cakes (*tempe*) on the side.
- This dish tastes best when served at room temperature or slightly warm.

# CREAMY LONG BEAN SALAD
## (JUKUT ANTUNGAN)

The rich, flavourful coconut cream dressing is a little spicy from the fried bird's eye chillies and deeply aromatic because of the crisp-fried shallots and garlic.

### Ingredients

| | |
|---|---|
| Long (snake) or winged beans | 600 g (1 lb 5 oz), or any crisp vegetable |
| Vegetable spice paste (see pg 8) | 150 g (5 oz) |
| Coconut cream | 125 ml (4 fl oz / $^1/_2$ cup) |
| Vegetable or chicken stock (see pg 10) | 125 ml (4 fl oz / $^1/_2$ cup) |
| Crisp-fried garlic | 2 Tbsp |
| Bird's eye chillies | 3, finely sliced and fried until golden |
| Lime juice | 2 Tbsp |
| Salt | a pinch or to taste |
| Ground black pepper | a pinch or to taste |
| Crisp-fried shallots | 2 Tbsp |

Step-By-Step

If not ready-made, prepare crisp-fried shallots and garlic slices first, then blanch long beans. Set both aside with grated coconut.

Combine blended spice paste and remaining coconut cream. Add chopped kaffir lime leaves and extra black pepper for extra fragrance if desired.

Just before serving, put all ingredients into a large bowl and mix well with dressing, then transfer to serving bowls.

### Method

- Cut beans of choice into 0.5-cm ($^1/_4$-inch) pieces, then blanch to soften. Drain and set aside.
- Combine spice paste and half the coconut cream in a stone mortar or blender (processor) and grind very fine. Transfer to a saucepan.
- To saucepan, add stock and remaining coconut cream. Bring to a quick boil, then remove from heat and leave to cool.
- Put all ingredients except crisp-fried shallots into a large bowl and mix well. Adjust to taste with salt and pepper.
- Serve garnished with crisp-fried shallots.

Sauté prawns in spice paste until evenly coated and colour changes from grey to whitish pink, indicating that prawns are nearly cooked.

Stir in stock and coconut cream, then simmer for 1 minute. This allows the 2 ingredients to heat through and the prawns to cook completely.

Prepare all remaining salad ingredients and set aside until ready to serve, then toss together and with dressing until well mixed.

# VEGETABLE AND PRAWN SALAD
## (*LAWAR UDANG*)

This salad of crunchy vegetables and succulent prawns with a deliciously creamy coconut dressing is sure to whet the appetite.

### Ingredients

| | |
|---|---|
| Vegetable of choice | 400 g (13$^{1}/_{2}$ oz), sliced and blanched (use firm vegetables like green papayas, long (snake) beans, bitter gourd, etc.) |
| Grated coconut | 120 g (4 oz), roasted |
| Crisp-fried shallots | 2 Tbsp + more for garnishing |
| Crisp-fried garlic | 2 Tbsp |
| Red chillies | 2, large, halved, seeded and finely sliced |
| Kaffir lime leaves | 2–3, finely chopped |
| Salt | to taste |
| Ground black pepper | to taste |

### Dressing

| | |
|---|---|
| Cooking oil | 2 Tbsp |
| Seafood spice paste (see pg 8) | 2 Tbsp |
| Prawns (shrimps) | 250 g (9 oz), shelled and deveined |
| Salt | to taste |
| Ground black pepper | to taste |
| Chicken stock (see pg 10) | 125 ml (4 fl oz / $^{1}/_{2}$ cup) |
| Coconut cream | 125 ml (4 fl oz / $^{1}/_{2}$ cup) |
| Lime juice | 2 Tbsp |

### Method

- Slice vegetables into desired serving size pieces. Blanch to soften, then drain and set aside.
- Prepare dressing. Heat oil in a heavy saucepan. Add spice paste and sauté until fragrant.
- Season prawns with salt and pepper, then add to spice paste. Sauté until colour changes.
- Stir in stock and coconut cream. Bring to the boil and simmer for 1 minute.
- Adjust to taste with salt and pepper and lime juice. Remove from heat and leave to cool to room temperature.
- Into a large bowl, put all ingredients and mix well. Serve garnished with crisp-fried shallots.

Season minced duck with salt and pepper to taste before adding to spice paste in pan.

Add stock and coconut cream and leave to cook for 1 minute, then adjust to taste with more seasoning if preferred.

Just before serving, combine all ingredients in a large bowl and toss with cooled dressing.

# MINCED DUCK AND GREEN PAPAYA SALAD
## (LAWAR KWIR)

A delightful salad of juicy minced duck and crunchy green papaya.

### Ingredients

| | |
|---|---|
| Green papaya | 400 g (13¹/₂ oz), peeled, halved, seeded, sliced into fine strips and blanched |
| Grated coconut | 150 g (5 oz), lightly roasted |
| Palm sugar | 1 Tbsp, finely grated |
| Crisp-fried garlic | 2 Tbsp |
| Crisp-fried shallots | 2 Tbsp + more for garnishing |
| Red chillies | 2, large, halved, seeded, finely sliced and fried until golden |
| Bird's eye chillies | 2–3, finely sliced and fried until golden |
| Kaffir lime leaves | 2–3, finely chopped |

### Dressing

| | |
|---|---|
| Cooking oil | 2 Tbsp |
| Basic spice paste (see pg 8) | 2 Tbsp |
| Minced duck meat | 300 g (10 oz), or giblets (heart, liver and stomach) |
| Salt | to taste |
| Ground black pepper | to taste |
| Chicken or duck stock (see pg 10) | 125 ml (4 fl oz / ¹/₂ cup) |
| Coconut cream | 125 ml (4 fl oz / ¹/₂ cup) |
| Lime juice | 2 Tbsp |

### Method

- Prepare dressing. Heat oil in a heavy saucepan. Add spice paste and sauté until fragrant.
- Season minced duck with salt and pepper, then add to spice paste. Continue to sauté until meat changes colour.
- Add stock and coconut cream. Bring to a quick boil and simmer for 1 minute. Adjust to taste with salt, pepper and lime juice.
- Remove from heat and leave to cool to room temperature.
- To prepare salad, combine all ingredients in a large bowl and mix well with cooled dressing.
- Garnish as desired with crisp-fried shallots and serve.

# JACKFRUIT AND PORK SALAD
## (LAWAR NANGKA)

A substantial salad of young jackfruit flavoured with meat juices from a pork-based dressing.

### Ingredients

| | |
|---|---|
| Young jackfruit | 400 g (13¹/₂ oz), peeled, sliced, boiled in salted water until cooked, cooled and roughly chopped |
| Grated coconut | 200 g (7 oz), lightly roasted |
| Crisp-fried garlic | 2 Tbsp |
| Crisp-fried shallots | 2 Tbsp + more for garnishing |
| Red chillies | 2, large, halved seeded, cut into fine strips and fried until golden |
| Bird's eye chillies | 4–6, finely sliced and fried until golden |
| Basic spice paste (see pg 8) | 2 Tbsp |
| Salt | to taste |
| Crushed black peppercorns | to taste |
| Kaffir lime juice | 1 Tbsp |

### Dressing

| | |
|---|---|
| Boned pork neck, shoulder or brisket | 250 g (9 oz), minced, or any meat of choice |
| Basic spice paste (see pg 8) | 2 Tbsp, or according to meat of choice |
| Kaffir lime leaves | 2–3, chopped |
| Salt | a pinch |
| Crushed black peppercorns | a pinch |
| Banana leaves | 6, each 18 x 12 cm (7 x 5 inches), or corn husks, greaseproof paper or aluminium foil |

Young jackfruit is used here in its entirety after peeling, premature seeds and membranes included.

Another way of preparing the parcels for steaming is to secure the ends with bamboo skewers or cocktail sticks instead of just folding them down.

Use a fork to break up cooked mince so that it returns to its original form.

*Step-By-Step*

### Method

- Combine jackfruit, grated coconut, fried garlic, shallots, chillies and basic spice paste in a large bowl. Mix well and set aside.
- Prepare dressing. Combine pork with basic spice paste, lime leaves, salt and pepper. Mix well.

- Spoon minced mixture onto the centre of banana leaf rectangle. Fold in 2 long sides to enclose ingredients, then fold down the ends so the weight of the parcel rests on them. Repeat until ingredients are used up.
- Steam parcels for 20 minutes or until cooked. Remove and leave to cool to room temperature.

- Open cooled parcels and use a fork to break up meat.
- Add cooked minced pork to jackfruit mixture. Season to taste with salt, pepper and lime juice.
- Garnish with crisp-fried shallots and serve with prawn (shrimp) crackers if desired.

Grilled Fish in Banana Leaf (*Pesan Be Pasih*)

Lobster Braised in Coconut Milk (*Udang Pantung Kuning*)

Marinated Grilled Seafood (*Be Pasih Mepanggang*)

Marinated Mahi-mahi Steamed in Bamboo (*Timbungan*)

Minced Seafood Saté (*Sate Lilit Ikan*)

Tuna Salad with Shallot and Lemon Grass Dressing (*Sambel Be Tongkol*)

Feel fillet for fine bones, usually near the middle, and remove, if any, before cutting into cubes.

Mix fish cubes with spice paste until evenly coated.

Fold one-third of banana leaf over ingredients and press down to pack in ingredients before rolling up.

# GRILLED FISH IN BANANA LEAF
## (PESAN BE PASIH)

With only light cooking, this dish of mildly spiced fish is delicious and easy to prepare.

### Ingredients

| | |
|---|---|
| Fish fillet | 600 g (1 lb 5 oz), skinned, boned and cut into 1.5-cm ($^3$/4-in) cubes |
| Salt | a pinch |
| Crushed black peppercorns | a pinch |
| Seafood spice paste (see pg 8) | 125 g (4$^1$/2 oz) |
| *Salam* leaves | 4 |
| Banana leaves | 4, cut into 15-cm (6-in) squares |
| Tomatoes | 2, quartered |
| Lemon basil | 8 sprigs |
| Bamboo skewers or cocktail sticks | |

### Method

- Season fish with salt and pepper, then mix with seafood spice paste.
- Place 1 *salam* leaf onto the centre of a banana leaf. Top with 1 Tbsp marinated fish, 2 tomato pieces and 2 sprigs lemon basil.
- Fold one-third of banana leaf over ingredients and roll up tightly. Secure ends with skewers or cocktail sticks. Repeat until ingredients are used up.
- Cover parcels and leave to marinate in a cool place for 30 minutes.

- Parcels can be cooked in a few ways— steamed over rapidly boiling water for 7 minutes, grilled over very low heat for 9 minutes or baked in an oven preheated to 180°C/350°F for 9 minutes.
- Alternatively, steam for 4 minutes, then place over charcoal heat or under a grill and cook for 3 minutes until banana leaves are evenly browned.
- Perhaps the most common way in Bali is to place the parcels on a dry, heated iron plate or a frying pan (skillet) and cook until done.

- It is important that the parcels are not overcooked because the fish dries out very quickly. Instead, undercook them slightly, then leave them to rest in a warm place for 5 minutes to cook in the residual heat.

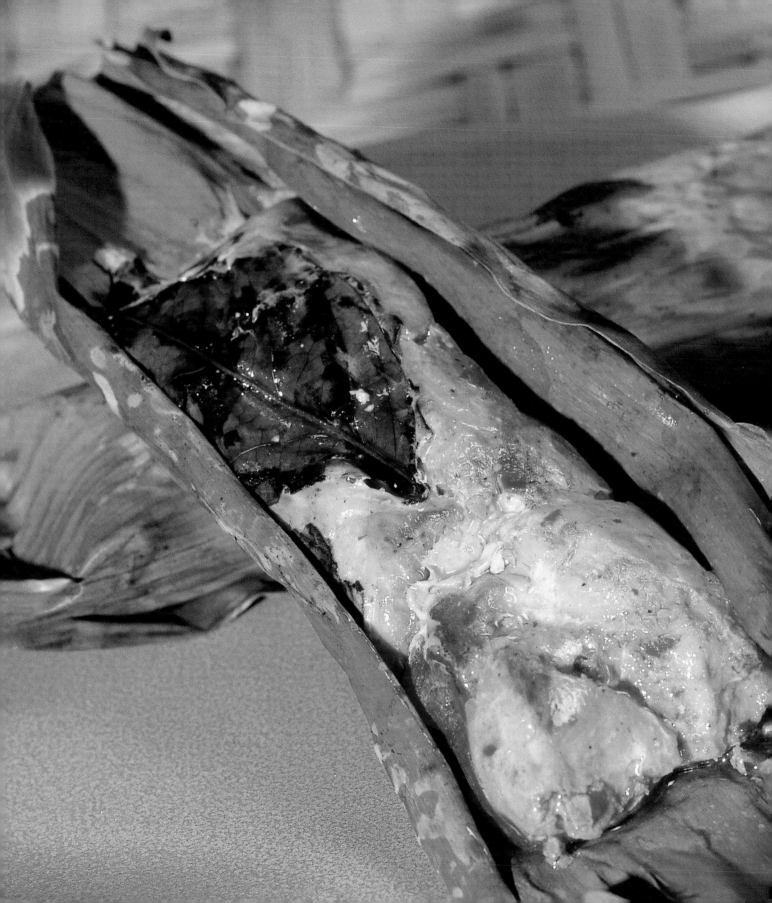

It is important to transfer cooked lobster to ice water to cool because the skin of the meat will then separate from the shell for easier extraction later.

Sauté lobster shell pieces until they are well coated with the spice paste before adding stock.

The repeated process of simmering away the stock and topping up with more is called glazing. The effect is that the sauce will have an appetising glaze at the end of cooking.

Step-By-Step

# LOBSTER BRAISED IN COCONUT MILK
## (UDANG PANTUNG KUNING)

Succulent lobster accompanied by a creamy, aromatic sauce, this richly flavoured dish is well worth the time and effort required to prepare it.

### Ingredients

| | |
|---|---|
| Lobsters | 4, medium, each about 500 g (1 lb 1$^{1}$/$_{2}$ oz) |
| Vegetable oil | 1 Tbsp |
| Seafood spice paste (see pg 8) | 125 g (4$^{1}$/$_{2}$ oz) |
| Lemon grass | 1 stalk, bruised |
| Kaffir lime leaves | 2, bruised |
| Bird's eye chillies | 3 |
| Chicken or fish stock (see pg 10) | 1.25 litres (2 pints / 5 cups) |
| Coconut milk | 250 ml (8 fl oz / 1 cup) |
| Lime juice | 1 Tbsp |
| Salt | to taste |
| Crushed black peppercorns | a pinch |

### Court Bouillon

| | |
|---|---|
| Water | 5 litres (8 pints / 20 cups) |
| Sea salt | 200 g (7 oz) |
| Kaffir lime leaves | 3, bruised |
| Limes | 2, sliced |

### Method

- Bring court bouillon ingredients to a rapid boil. Plunge lobsters, head first, into liquid.
- When liquid returns to the boil, simmer for 2 minutes more, then remove and plunge into ice water to cool.
- Halve each lobster lengthways using a sharp knife. Remove tail meat, trim off loose bits and set aside.
- Separate claws and legs from lobster body. Halve them and extract all the meat. Set aside.

- Chop lobster shells into walnut-size chunks with a cleaver. Set aside.
- Heat oil in heavy saucepan. Add spice paste, lemon grass, lime leaves and chillies. Sauté over medium heat for 2 minutes.
- Add lobster shells and sauté until shells are evenly coated with spice paste.
- Mix in 250 ml (8 fl oz / 1 cup) stock, bring to the boil and simmer until stock is almost completely evaporated.
- Add another 250 ml stock and repeat process. If total simmering time was less

than 20 minutes, repeat process with extra stock. Ideally, the process should be repeated 5 times.
- Pour in coconut milk, return to the boil and simmer over very low heat for 1 minute. Strain sauce through a fine sieve. Discard shells.
- In a separate saucepan, combine lobster tail, meat and sauce. Return to the boil and simmer for 1 minute.
- Season to taste with lime juice, salt and pepper. Serve.

Mix assorted seafood with lime juice, salt, pepper and spice paste. Leave to season.

Just before grilling, whether fish or assorted seafood, brush on a little basting liquid first.

When grilling over charcoal heat, turn and baste frequently to prevent the seafood from drying out and the spices from burning.

# MARINATED GRILLED SEAFOOD
## (BE PASIH MEPANGGANG)

The combination of sweet seafood juices and a smoky charcoal-grilled flavour makes this a memorable dish.

### Ingredients

| | |
|---|---|
| Assorted seafood | 1 kg (2 lb 3 oz), use fish fillets, prawns (shrimps), clams, mussels, etc., or 1 whole fish, 1 kg (2 lb 3 oz), use snapper, trevally, mackerel, etc. |
| Lime juice | 2 Tbsp |
| Salt | 1 tsp |
| Black peppercorns | 1 tsp, finely crushed |
| Seafood spice paste (see pg 8) | 200 g (7 oz) |

### Basting Paste (combined)

| | |
|---|---|
| Seafood spice paste | 125 g (4 1/2 oz) |
| Vegetable oil | 125 ml (4 fl oz / 1/2 cup) |

### Method

- If using assorted seafood, mix well with lime juice, salt, pepper and spice paste. Leave to marinate.
- If using whole fish, halve butterfly style; start at the head and work towards the tail. Make 4 slits, each about 1-cm (1/2-inch) deep, on the side with the bones. The seasoning will penetrate better and the fish will cook more evenly.

- Season both sides of fish with lime juice salt and pepper. Evenly spread spice paste all over.
- Brush assorted seafood or whole fish with a little basting paste before grilling over medium charcoal heat. Turn and baste frequently.

- Serve with white rice accompanied by desired portions of spiced tomato sauce (sambel tomat) and shallot and lemon grass dressing (sambel matah) (see pg 9) on the side.

# MARINATED MAHI-MAHI STEAMED IN BAMBOO
## (*TIMBUNGAN*)

For this dish, the Balinese often replace fish with eel, crab or prawns (shrimps). If bamboo is unavailable, use banana leaves or corn husks as wrappers, then steam or charcoal-grill parcels to cook.

S
t
e
p
-
B
y
-
S
t
e
p

After mixing fish with spice paste, lime juice, salt and pepper, place in the refrigerator to marinate.

### Ingredients

| | |
|---|---|
| Firm fish fillet | 600 g (1 lb 5 oz), skinned, cleaned and diced, use mahi-mahi, snapper or mackerel |
| Seafood spice paste (see pg 8) | 125 g (4$^{1}/_{2}$ oz) |
| Lime juice | 1 Tbsp |
| Salt | a pinch |
| Crushed black peppercorns | a pinch |
| Grated coconut | 100 g (3$^{1}/_{2}$ oz) |
| Coconut cream | 125 ml (4 fl oz / $^{1}/_{2}$ cup) |
| Crisp-fried shallots | 2 Tbsp |
| Crisp-fried garlic | 2 Tbsp |
| Bird's eye chillies | 2, finely chopped |
| Chopped palm sugar | 1 tsp |
| Chopped kaffir lime leaves | $^{1}/_{2}$ tsp |

Fill bamboo cavity with ingredients until they are quite tightly packed together.

### Stuffing

| | |
|---|---|
| *Salam* leaves | 4 |
| Tomatoes | 2, halved and sliced |
| Lemon basil | 8 sprigs |
| Bamboo segments | 1 large, or 4 small, scrubbed clean and steamed empty for 30 minutes |

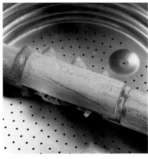

Place covered bamboo into a steamer over rapidly boiling water to cook ingredients inside.

### Method

- Combine fish, spice paste, lime juice, salt and pepper in a bowl. Mix well and leave to marinate for 10 minutes in the refrigerator.
- Add all remaining ingredients to fish and mix well.

- Place 1 *salam* leaf at one end of prepared bamboo segment. Add on some fish followed by a slice of tomato and basil, then repeat order of ingredients until cavity is filled.
- If using 4 small bamboo segments, repeat stuffing process with remaining three segments.

- Replace bamboo cover and steam for about 15 minutes. Alternatively, place bamboo directly onto hot charcoal and cook for 10 minutes.

Use only fresh fish. Frozen fish will not work because the resulting paste will be too watery and will slide off the lemon grass stalks or skewers later.

To prepare cleaned lemon grass stalks for use as saté skewers, trim off their leafy top and root ends.

To prepare saté for grilling, mould 1 rounded (heaped) Tbsp of minced fish mixture as shown around lemon grass stalk or skewer.

Step-By-Step

# MINCED SEAFOOD SATÉ
## (SATE LILIT IKAN)

An interesting variation of saté, which is usually meat-based, seafood saté makes for a lighter meal and more delicate flavours.

### Ingredients

| | |
|---|---|
| Snapper fillet | 600 g (1 lb 5 oz), skinned, boned, finely minced |
| Freshly grated coconut | 125 g (4$^1$/$_2$ oz) |
| Coconut cream | 125 ml (4 fl oz / $^1$/$_2$ cup) |
| Seafood spice paste (see pg 8) | 125 g (4$^1$/$_2$ oz) |
| Bird's eye chillies | 3–5, very finely chopped |
| Kaffir lime leaves | 5, finely chopped |
| Ground black pepper | a pinch |
| Salt | a pinch |
| Palm sugar | 1 Tbsp |
| Lemon grass stalks or large bamboo skewers | |

### Method

- Combine all ingredients except lemon grass or bamboo skewers and mix thoroughly until a uniformly sticky paste results.
- Mould 1 rounded (heaped) Tbsp mixture around the trimmed bulbous end of a lemon grass stalk or a bamboo skewer. Repeat until ingredients are used up.
- Grill over very hot charcoal until golden brown.
- For variation, replace half the amount of minced fish used with minced prawns (shrimps).

# TUNA SALAD WITH SHALLOTS AND LEMON GRASS DRESSING
## (SAMBEL BE TONGKOL)

Serve this at room temperature with steamed rice, or as a cocktail snack on top of deep-fried prawn or seafood crackers (*krupuk*).

### Ingredients

| | |
|---|---|
| Tuna steaks | 4, each about 150 g (5 oz) |
| Seafood spice paste (see pg 8) | 65 g (2$^1$/$_2$ oz) |
| Salt | $^1$/$_2$ tsp or more to taste |
| Ground black pepper | a pinch or more to taste |
| Lime juice | 1 Tbsp |
| Vegetable oil | 2 Tbsp |
| Shallot and lemon grass dressing (*sambel matah*) (see pg 9) | 125 g (4$^1$/$_2$ oz) |
| Kaffir lime leaf | 1 or to taste, finely chopped |
| Crisp-fried shallots | 2 Tbsp |
| Red chilli (optional) | 1, sliced and fried until golden |
| Lime (optional) | 1, cut into wedges and seeded |

**Step-By-Step**

Cook seasoned tuna steaks over medium heat until desired doneness is achieved. Turn frequently.

For added fragrance and flavour, reserve lime halves after squeezing for juice and mix with flaked tuna.

When ingredients are well mixed, transfer to individual serving plates or bowls.

### Method

- Season tuna steaks with seafood spice paste, salt, pepper and lime juice.
- Heat oil in frying pan (skillet). Fry tuna steaks over medium high heat, turning frequently until desired doneness is achieved; do not overcook. Dish out and set aside to cool.
- In a mixing bowl, flake tuna into small chunks. Add shallot and lemon grass dressing and kaffir lime leaf. Mix well. Adjust to taste with salt and pepper.
- Transfer tossed ingredients to a serving plate or bowl. Garnish with crisp-fried shallots and fried chilli slices, if used. Serve with lime wedges, if desired.

MEAT & POULTRY

After mixing meat with spice paste, leave in a cool place to marinate for 1 hour.

Fry marinated meat with spices over medium heat until meat changes colour, which means that the surfaces are cooked.

Add in coconut milk last and simmer until meat is tender. Should sauce reduce too much, add a little chicken stock and stir.

**Step-By-Step**

# BALINESE LAMB STEW
## (*KAMBING MEKUAH*)

In Indonesia, goat meat or chevon is also used for this dish. Goat meat has a strong gamy flavour, which is why very pungent spices and vinegar are added to counter it. This recipe also works well with any kind of game or game birds.

### Ingredients

| | |
|---|---|
| Boned lamb leg or shoulder | 800 g (1 lb 5 oz), cut into 2-cm (1-inch) cubes |
| Basic spice paste (see pg 8) | 250 g (9 oz) |
| Cooking oil | 2 Tbsp |
| Coriander seeds | 1 Tbsp, crushed |
| Cardamoms | 12, bruised and ground |
| Lemon grass | 1 stalk, bruised |
| *Salam* leaves | 3 |
| Chicken stock (see pg 10) | 1 litre (1$^3/_5$ pints / 4 cups) |
| Rice vinegar | 1 Tbsp |
| Coconut milk | 250 ml (8 fl oz / 1 cup) |
| Salt | a pinch or to taste |
| Crushed black peppercorns | a pinch |

### Method

- Combine meat and spice paste in a large bowl and mix well. Leave to marinate in a cool place for 1 hour.
- Heat oil in a heavy saucepan. Add marinated meat, coriander seeds, cardamoms, lemon grass and *salam* leaves. Sauté over medium heat until meat changes colour.
- Add half the chicken stock and vinegar. Bring to the boil, reduce heat and simmer until meat is almost cooked. Frequently top up with more stock as it evaporates.
- Pour in coconut milk. Return to the boil, reduce heat to very low and simmer until meat is tender and sauce shiny and creamy.

# BRAISED BEEF IN COCONUT MILK
## (BE SAMPI MEMBASE BALI)

The sauce of this hearty beef stew is best savoured with plain steamed rice. A good stewing pan, which should be wide and shallow, is important to the success of the dish.

### Ingredients

| | |
|---|---|
| Vegetable oil | 2 Tbsp |
| Beef spice paste (see pg 8) | 250 g (9 oz) |
| Beef shoulder, brisket or neck | 800 g (1 lb 5 oz), cut in 2.5-cm (1-inch) cubes |
| Lemon grass | 2 stalks, bruised |
| *Salam* leaves | 2 |
| Galangal (*laos*) | 70 g (2½ oz), peeled, sliced and bruised |
| Beef or chicken stock (see pg 10) | 1 litre (1³/5 pints / 4 cups) |
| Coconut milk | 1 litre (1³/5 pints / 4 cups) |
| Salt | to taste |
| Cracked black peppercorns | to taste |
| Crisp-fried shallots for garnishing | |

S t e p - B y - S t e p

It is important to fry the spice paste until fragrant before adding the meat. This maximises the flavour and aroma imparted to the meat.

If preferred, knot the bruised lemon grass stalks for better presentation and to prevent the fibres from separating during cooking.

Never add so much stock as to completely immerse the meat. In the case of stewing, the liquid should only cover the lower half of the meat.

### Method

- Heat oil in a heavy sauce- or stewing pan. Add spice paste and fry over low heat for 2 minutes or until fragrant.
- Add beef and sauté until meat changes colour.
- Add lemon grass, *salam* leaves and galangal. Sauté for 2 minutes more.
- Add half the stock. Bring to the boil, reduce heat and simmer until meat is almost cooked. Regularly top up with more stock as it evaporates.
- Pour in coconut milk and return to the boil. Simmer until meat is tender and sauce thickens. Season to taste with salt and pepper.
- Serve garnished with crisp-fried shallots.

# BRAISED PORK RIBS WITH YOUNG JACKFRUIT
## (*BALUNG NANGKA*)

The unusual combination of pork ribs and jackfruit is enhanced by the subtle fragrances of lemon grass, *salam* leaves and ginger.

### Ingredients

| | |
|---|---|
| Pork ribs | 1 kg (2 lb 3 oz), cut into 3-cm (1¹/₂-inch) pieces |
| Basic spice paste (see pg 8) | 325 g (11¹/₂ oz) |
| Cooking oil | 2 Tbsp |
| Lemon grass | 2 stalks, bruised |
| *Salam* leaves | 4 |
| Ginger | 50 g, peeled, sliced and bruised |
| Red chillies | 2, large, left whole |
| Chicken stock (see pg 10) | 1.5 litres (2²/₅ pints / 6 cups) |
| Young jackfruit | 400 g, peeled, cleaned and cut into 2.5 x 1-cm (1 x ¹/₂-inch) pieces |
| Salt | to taste |
| Crushed black peppercorns | to taste |
| Kaffir lime leaves (optional) | 1–2, finely chopped, for garnishing |

**Step-By-Step**

Cover pork ribs with spice paste well. This ensures even flavouring and colouring.

Pan-fry pork ribs to lightly cook the surfaces and seal in the juices before adding stock to braise.

Separately cook the jackfruit pieces in salted water before adding to pan to braise with pork ribs.

### Method

- Season pork ribs with 125 g (4¹/₂ oz) spice paste and set aside in cool place for 1 hour.
- Heat oil in a heavy stewing pan. Add remaining spice paste and sauté until fragrant.
- Add pork ribs, lemon grass, *salam* leaves, ginger and chillies. Continue to sauté until pork ribs change colour.

- Pour in half the chicken stock. Bring to the boil and simmer until ribs are almost cooked. Top up with more stock as it evaporates.
- Meanwhile, cook jackfruit. Bring 3 litres (5⁴/₅ pints / 12 cups) of salted water to the boil and add jackfruit.
- Return to the boil and simmer for about 15 minutes or until almost cooked.

- Drain and transfer jackfruit into ice water to cool, then drain well.
- Add jackfruit to pork ribs and simmer until ribs are tender.
- Season to taste with salt and black pepper. Serve garnished with chopped kaffir lime leaves, if used.

To prepare banana leaves for use, first wipe them clean, then soften them either over heat or in some hot water.

At one end, bring up the lower, folded edge so it is perpendicular to the base and forms 2 flaps. Fold flaps in towards the centre. Repeat with other end.

Holding the flaps firmly in place, take a banana leaf strip and wrap it around the centre of the parcel.

# MINCED PORK AND MUSHROOMS IN BANANA LEAF (*PESAN BABI-WONG*)

This recipe also can be prepared with chicken or duck. Replace basic spice paste with that for chicken.

### Ingredients

| | |
|---|---|
| Pork shoulder or neck | 400 g (13½ oz), minced |
| Shiitake mushrooms | 100 g (3½ oz), diced |
| Basic spice paste (see pg 8) | 90 g (3 oz) |
| Bird's eye chillies | 4, sliced and fried until golden |
| Crisp-fried shallots | 2 Tbsp |
| Crisp-fried garlic | 1 Tbsp |
| Palm sugar | 1 tsp, chopped |
| Salt | a pinch |
| Crushed black peppercorns | a pinch |
| Coconut cream | 80 ml (2½ fl oz) |
| *Salam* leaves | 12 |
| Banana leaf squares | 12, each 12 x 12 cm (5 x 5 inches) |
| Banana leaf strips | 12, each 3.5 x 12 cm (1½ x 5 inches) |
| Bamboo skewers or cocktail sticks | |

### Method

- Mix minced pork, mushrooms, spice paste, chillies, fried shallots and garlic, palm sugar, salt, pepper and coconut cream together in a bowl until a smooth paste results.
- Place 1 *salam* leaf onto the centre of a banana leaf square. Top with 1 Tbsp of prepared meat mixture.
- Fold banana leaf in half by bringing 2 opposing edges together.
- Fold in ends as shown in Step 2, then wrap a banana leaf strip around the parcel as shown in Step 3.
- Secure with a bamboo skewer or cocktail stick and trim off excess leaf. Repeat until ingredients are used up.
- Steam parcels for about 10 minutes or until well cooked.
- Remove and unwrap to serve.

After sautéing for 2 minutes, shallots and garlic should be lightly browned.

After adding both soy sauces and crushed peppercorns, sauté for 1 minute to mix ingredients together.

Begin simmering with half the stock and whole chillies added. Gradually add more stock as it evaporates during cooking.

Step-By-Step

# PORK IN SWEET SOY SAUCE
## (BE CELENG BASE MANIS)

Tender cubes of pork are smothered in a thick, lip-smacking sauce that is mildly spicy but definitely whets the appetite.

### Ingredients

| | |
|---|---|
| Vegetable oil | 2 Tbsp |
| Shallots | 70 g (2¹/₂ oz), peeled and sliced |
| Garlic | 50 g (2 oz), peeled and sliced |
| Boned pork shoulder or neck | 800 g (1 lb 5 oz), cut into 2-cm (1-inch) cubes |
| Ginger | 50 g (2 oz), peeled and sliced |
| Sweet soy sauce (*kecap manis*) | 4 Tbsp |
| Salty soy sauce (*kecap asin*) | 2 Tbsp |
| Crushed black peppercorns | a pinch |
| Chicken stock (see pg 10) | 1 litre (1³/₅ pints / 4 cups) |
| Bird's eye chillies | 6–10, left whole |
| Red chillies | 2–3, large, left whole |

### Method

- Heat oil in a heavy saucepan. Add shallots and garlic and sauté over medium heat for 2 minutes or until lightly coloured.
- Add pork and ginger. Sauté, still over medium heat, for 2 minutes more.
- Add both soy sauces and black pepper. Sauté for 1 minute.
- Pour in half the chicken stock, add both chillies and simmer over medium heat for about 1 hour. Top up with more stock as it evaporates.
- When done, there should be very little sauce left and the meat should be shiny and dark brown in colour.

# PORK SATÉ
## (SATE ASAM CELENG)

Contrary to most preparations of grilled saté, Balinese saté is not served with a creamy peanut sauce but a mixture of salt and chopped chillies.

### Ingredients

| | |
|---|---|
| Pork tenderloin or loin | 600 g (1 lb 5 oz), cut into 1 x 0.5-cm (½ x ¼-inch) pieces |
| Basic spice paste (see pg 8) | 125 g (4½ oz) |
| Bird's eye chillies | 3–5, chopped |
| Palm sugar | 1 Tbsp |
| Salt | a pinch |
| Bamboo or saté skewers | |

Step-By-Step

If pork is not your meat of choice, replace with chicken or beef and also the respective spice paste (see pg 8).

After threading 4–6 pieces of meat onto a skewer, push them together so they are tightly packed at one end, covering about 5 cm (2 inches) of the skewer.

Always serve saté directly from the grill to the plate. Never cook satés in advance as they will loose a lot of juice and with that, become tough and flavourless.

### Method

- Combine all ingredients except skewers in a bowl and mix well.
- Thread 4–6 pieces of meat onto a skewer and push them together towards one end of skewer. Repeat until ingredients are used up.
- Cover saté and leave to marinate in the refrigerator for 1 hour.
- Grill over very hot charcoal until desired doneness is reached. Serve immediately.
- Whenever possible, grill over charcoal so hot that it will almost burn the skewers. Done this way, the palm sugar in the marinade will caramelise and provide added flavour.

# CHICKEN IN SPICED COCONUT MILK

## (BE SIAP BASE KALAS)

If preferred, include some vegetables such as tomatoes or baby carrots for a more balanced meal.

### Ingredients

| | |
|---|---|
| Chicken thighs (legs) | 800 g (1 lb 5 oz) |
| Vegetable oil | 1 Tbsp |
| Chicken spice paste (see pg 8) | 250 g (9 oz) |
| Lemon grass | 1 stalk, bruised |
| *Salam* leaf | 1 |
| Kaffir lime leaf | 1 |
| Chicken stock (see pg 10) | 250 ml (8 fl oz / 1 cup) |
| Coconut cream | 250 ml (8 fl oz / 1 cup) |
| Salt | a pinch or to taste |
| Finely crushed black peppercorns | a pinch |
| Lime juice | to taste |
| Crisp-fried shallots for garnishing | |
| Finely chopped kaffir lime leaves for garnishing | |

Step-By-Step

After sautéing for 2 minutes, spice paste should appear crumbly but still moist. Add lemon grass and *salam* and kaffir lime leaves.

After adding in chicken pieces, sauté to coat them well with the spice paste.

If sauce becomes too thick during cooking, stir in a little chicken stock.

### Method

- Wash and drain chicken. Debone and cut fillets into 2.5-cm (1-inch) pieces. Set aside.
- Heat oil in a heavy saucepan. Add spice paste and sauté over low heat for 2 minutes or until fragrant.
- Add lemon grass, *salam* and kaffir lime leaves. Sauté for 1 minute.

- Add chicken and sauté for 2 minutes or until meat changes colour.
- Pour in chicken stock, bring to the boil and simmer for 1 minute.
- Add coconut cream and return to the boil. Simmer over very low heat until chicken is cooked and sauce thickens.

- Season to taste with salt and pepper and fresh lime juice.
- Garnish with crisp-fried shallots and kaffir lime leaves. Serve.

Cut each spring chicken into 8 similarly sized pieces. This is so that they will cook more evenly in the same amount of time.

Measure up 500 ml (16 fl oz / 2 cups) of sauce and combine with rice flour using a balloon whisk.

Lower each piece of floured chicken into the rich batter and coat evenly.

# FRIED CHICKEN
## (*SIAP MEGORENG*)

An old favourite, fried chicken is given an aromatic Balinese twist here.

### Ingredients

| | |
|---|---|
| Spring chickens | 4, each about 800 g (1 lb 5 oz) |
| Chicken spice paste (see pg 8) | 250 g (9 oz) |
| Salt | a pinch + more to taste |
| Crushed black peppercorns | a pinch + more to taste |
| Vegetable oil | 2 Tbsp |
| Lemon grass | 2 stalks, bruised |
| *Salam* leaves | 3 |
| Bird's eye chillies | 3–4, bruised |
| Kaffir lime leaves | 2, bruised |
| Chicken stock (see pg 10) | 1 litre (1³/5 pints / 4 cups) |
| Coconut milk | 250 ml (8 fl oz / 1 cup) |
| Rice flour | 100 g (3¹/2 oz) |

### Method

- Cut each chicken into 8 pieces and season with half the spice paste and a pinch each of salt and pepper. Cover and leave to marinate in refrigerator.
- Heat oil in a heavy saucepan. Add remaining spice paste, lemon grass, *salam* leaves, bird's eye chillies and kaffir lime leaves. Sauté over medium heat for 2 minutes.
- Add stock and bring to the boil, then add coconut milk and bring to a simmer.

- Add chicken, reduce heat and simmer until 75 per cent cooked. Turn chicken frequently when cooking.
- Leave chicken in the sauce to cool to room temperature, then remove and drain well.
- Combine 500 ml (16 fl oz / 2 cups) of sauce with rice flour and mix until a smooth batter results. Season to taste with salt and pepper.

- Dust chicken pieces with flour, then coat with batter.
- Deep-fry at 160–170°C/320–340°F until golden and crispy. Drain and serve with lemon wedges if preferred.

# GRILLED CHICKEN
## (*SIAP MEPANGGANG*)

The smoky flavour of charcoal-grilled meat is inimitably inviting and appetising, but even without it, the chicken here is flavoursome enough to be gripping.

### Ingredients

| | |
|---|---|
| Spring chickens | 4, each about 800 g (1 3/4 lb) |
| Chicken spice paste (see pg 8) | 250 g (9 oz) |
| Salt | a pinch or to taste |
| Crushed black peppercorns | a pinch or to taste |
| Vegetable oil | 2 Tbsp |
| Lemon grass | 2 stalks, bruised |
| *Salam* leaves | 3 |
| Bird's eye chillies | 3–4, bruised |
| Kaffir lime leaves | 2, bruised |
| Chicken stock (see pg 10) | 1 litre (1 3/5 pints / 4 cups) |
| Coconut cream | 250 ml (8 fl oz / 1 cup) |

### Basting Liquid (combined)

| | |
|---|---|
| Chicken spice paste | 125 g (4 1/2 oz) |
| Vegetable oil | 125 ml (4 fl oz / 1/2 cup) |

After seasoning with salt, pepper and half the spice paste, put chicken into a covered container and leave to marinate in the refrigerator.

When chicken is 75 per cent cooked, turn off heat and leave chicken to cool to room temperature in the sauce.

For alternative presentation, leave chicken whole and slit along its back bone to open up and flatten, butterfly style.

### Method

- Cut chicken up into similarly sized, smaller pieces.
- Season chicken with half the spice paste, salt and pepper. Cover and leave to marinate in refrigerator.
- Heat oil in a heavy saucepan. Add remaining spice paste, lemon grass, *salam* leaves, bird's eye chillies and kaffir lime leaves. Sauté over medium heat for 2 minutes.
- Pour in chicken stock and bring to the boil, then add coconut cream and bring to a simmer.
- Add chicken, reduce heat and simmer until 75 per cent cooked. Turn chicken frequently when cooking.
- Leave chicken in sauce to cool to room temperature, then remove and drain well. Reserve sauce.
- Grill chicken either in the oven or over very hot, glowing charcoal until cooked and golden brown. Baste frequently.
- Heat up reserved sauce and simmer until all the liquid is evaporated. The result is a delicious, oily dipping sauce to go with the grilled chicken.

# QUAIL'S EGGS IN SPICED TOMATO SAUCE
## (TELOR BASE LALAH)

A pleasantly creamy, spicy and tangy sauce blankets fried quail's eggs. This recipe can also be prepared with chicken's eggs.

### Ingredients

| | |
|---|---|
| Quail's eggs | 28 |
| Vegetable oil | 1 Tbsp + enough for deep-frying |
| Chicken spice paste (see pg 8) | 2 Tbsp |
| Spiced tomato sauce (see pg 9) | 4 Tbsp |
| Dried prawn (shrimp) paste (*terasi*) | 1/2 tsp, roasted and crumbled |
| Red chillies | 50 g (2 oz), large, seeded and sliced |
| Bird's eye chillies | 3–5, chopped |
| Chicken stock (see pg 10) | 250 ml (8 fl oz / 1 cup) |
| Coconut cream | 125 ml (4 fl oz / 1/2 cup) |
| Tomatoes | 100 g (3 1/2 oz), seeded and sliced |
| Lime juice | 1 Tbsp |
| Salt | a pinch or to taste |
| Crisp-fried shallots for garnishing | |
| Finely chopped kaffir lime leaves for garnishing | |

Step-By-Step

While deep-frying the eggs adds flavour and texture, it is not really necessary. Skip the step for a lighter, more digestible meal.

Fry spice and dried prawn pastes, tomato sauce and chillies together until fragrant before adding stock. The chillies may cause a little choking.

Add in coconut cream and tomatoes and simmer for just 1 minute before adding quail's eggs.

### Method

- Bring 3 litres (5 4/5 pints /12 cups) of heavily salted water to the boil. Gently add in quail's eggs and simmer for 5 minutes.
- Remove eggs and transfer to ice water to cool. This process loosens the skins of the hard-boiled eggs from the shells and allows for easier shelling.
- Drain and dry shelled eggs on absorbent paper towels.

- Deep-fry in medium-hot oil until eggs are golden. Drain eggs on absorbent paper towels.
- Heat 1 Tbsp oil in a saucepan. Add chicken spice paste, tomato sauce, dried prawn paste and chillies. Sauté until fragrant.
- Pour in chicken stock and bring to the boil. Simmer for 1 minute.

- Add coconut cream and tomato slices. Return to the boil and simmer for 1 minute more.
- Mix in quail's eggs. Return to the boil again and simmer for 2 minutes. Add more stock if sauce reduces and thickens too much.
- Season to taste with lime juice and salt. Garnish as desired and serve.

Be careful not to tear chicken's skin when stuffing mixture underneath.

Wrap the chicken in several layers of banana leaves to prevent any leakage of juices.

After wrapping, secure banana leaves with skewers as shown, then place the entire parcel into a steamer.

Step-By-Step

# ROAST CHICKEN IN BANANA LEAF
## (AYAM BETUTU)

Traditionally, the chicken was wrapped in layers of banana stem, not leaves. The thicker stem layers protected the chicken from searing hot coals and cooked the chicken with steam instead of charcoal heat.

### Ingredients

| | |
|---|---|
| Chicken | 1, 1.2–1.4 kg (2 lb 10 oz–3 lb) |
| Salt | a pinch + more for seasoning |
| Crushed black peppercorns | a pinch + more for seasoning |
| Shallots | 50 g (2 oz), peeled and sliced |
| Garlic | 25 g (1 oz), peeled and chopped |
| Turmeric | 50 g (2 oz), peeled and chopped |
| Lesser galangal (kencur) | 25 g (1 oz), cleaned and sliced |
| Galangal (laos) | 25 g (1 oz), peeled and sliced |
| Candlenuts | 25 g (1 oz), chopped |
| Bird's eye chillies | 5, finely sliced |
| Red chillies | 2, large, seeded and sliced |
| Lemon grass | 4 stalks, bruised, finely sliced and minced |
| Palm sugar | 25 g (1 oz), chopped |
| Cooking oil | 2 Tbsp |
| Tapioca (cassava) leaves | 200 g (7 oz), cleaned, blanched for 5 minutes and roughly chopped |
| | |
| Salam leaves | 2, left whole |
| Banana leaves for wrapping | |
| Bamboo or saté skewers | |

### Method

- Clean chicken thoroughly, then season inside and out with salt and pepper.
- Combine all ingredients except tapioca, salam and banana leaves, as well as skewers in a bowl. Mix well. Reserve and set aside one-quarter of mixture.
- To remaining three-quarters, add tapioca and salam leaves. Mix well again.

- Fill chicken's cavity with mixture, then seal opening with a bamboo or saté skewer.
- Stuff reserved mixture under chicken's skin, then wrap in several layers of banana leaves and secure with bamboo or saté skewers.

- Steam parcel for 35 minutes, then remove and open top layers of banana leaves.
- Transfer open parcel to an oven preheated to 180°C/350°F and roast for 30–40 minutes.
- Unwrap to serve.

# SHREDDED CHICKEN WITH CHILLIES AND LIME
## (*AYAM PELALAH*)

Aromatic and slightly tangy, this light chicken dish will make a decent meal for two with a vegetable dish and some steamed rice.

### Ingredients

| | |
|---|---|
| Chicken | 1 whole, 1.2–1.5 kg (2 lb 10 oz–3 lb) |
| Salt | a pinch + more for seasoning |
| Finely crushed black pepper | a pinch + more for seasoning |
| Chicken spice paste (see pg 8) | 250 g (9 oz) |
| *Salam* leaves | 2 |
| Lemon grass | 2 stalks, bruised |
| Kaffir lime leaves | 2 |
| Bamboo or saté skewers | |
| Spiced tomato sauce (see pg 9) | 45 g (1 1/2 oz) |
| Lime juice | 3 Tbsp |
| Crisp-fried shallots | 2 Tbsp |

### Basting Liquid (combined)

| | |
|---|---|
| Chicken spice paste | 250 g (9 oz) |
| Vegetable oil | 250 ml (8 fl oz / 1 cup) |

After stuffing chicken, close opening using a bamboo or saté skewer.

It is important to baste chicken frequently during roasting so that chicken remains moist and does not dry up or, worse, burn.

Skin cooled chicken, then shred meat finely. Discard skin. If desired, cut chicken into smaller pieces first for easier handling.

### Method

- Rub chicken inside and outside with salt and pepper.
- Stuff chicken's cavity with 3 Tbsp spice paste, *salam* leaves, lemon grass and kaffir lime leaves, then close opening with skewers.
- Rub outside of chicken evenly with remaining spice paste.
- Place chicken on a wire rack in an oven preheated to 220°C/430°F and roast for 10 minutes.
- Turn heat down to 160°C/325°F and roast chicken until done and juices run clear, basting frequently. Remove cooked chicken from oven and leave to cool to room temperature.
- Skin and debone cooled chicken and shred meat finely by hand. Reserve stuffing for making dressing later.
- Combine chicken shreds with spiced tomato sauce, lime juice, crisp-fried shallots and chicken stuffing. Mix well and season to taste.
- Serve at room temperature with steamed rice.
- For variation, deep-fry seasoned chicken shreds in medium-hot oil (170°C/340°F) until golden and crispy, then drain on paper towels. The Balinese call the resulting dish *abon ayam*.
- For another variation, replace the spiced tomato sauce with 4 Tbsp shallot and lemon grass dressing (see pg 9) for a light, fresh chicken salad the Balinese call *ayam sambel matah*.

Yellow Rice (*Nasi Kuning*)

Fried Rice with Chicken and Prawns (*Nasi Goreng*)

Rice Porridge with Chicken (*Bubur Ayam*)

Fried Noodles with Vegetables (*Mie Goreng*)

Clean rice well of impurities by washing in several changes of water, then soak in water for 5 minutes.

Remove turmeric dressing from heat and pour into a bowl, then add in rice and mix well.

When rice grains have amply absorbed the turmeric dressing as shown, it is ready for the second round of steaming.

S t e p - B y - S t e p

# YELLOW RICE
## (NASI KUNING)

*Nasi kuning* looks and smells great and generally goes well with stewed dishes. For a lighter meal, replace the 125 ml (4 fl oz / 1/2 cup) of coconut milk in this recipe with chicken stock.

### Ingredients

| | |
|---|---|
| Long grain rice | 250 g (9 oz), washed and drained |
| Vegetable oil | 1 Tbsp |
| Shallots | 50 g (2 oz), peeled and chopped |
| Garlic | 25 g (3/4 oz), peeled and chopped |
| Lemon grass | 1 stalk, bruised |
| *Salam* leaves | 2 |
| Screwpine (*pandan*) leaf | 1 |
| Chicken stock (see pg 10) | 375 ml (12 fl oz / 1 1/2 cups) |
| Turmeric | 30 g (1 oz), peeled, finely chopped, ground until fine with 60 ml (2 fl oz) water and strained |
| Coconut milk | 125 ml (4 fl oz / 1/2 cup) |
| Salt | a pinch or to taste |
| Ground black pepper | a pinch or to taste |

### Method

- Soak cleaned rice in fresh water for 5 minutes. Drain and steam for 25 minutes.
- Meanwhile, prepare dressing. Heat oil in a saucepan. Add shallots and garlic. Sauté for 1 minute.
- Add lemon grass and *salam* and screwpine leaves. Sauté for 1 minute.

- Pour in chicken stock and turmeric juice. Bring to the boil, reduce heat and simmer for 1 minute.
- Add coconut milk, return to the boil and simmer for 2 minutes. Season to taste with salt and pepper.
- Combine steamed rice and hot dressing in a large bowl. Mix well and set aside.

- When rice has absorbed the yellow liquid, return rice to steamer and steam for another 25 minutes or until rice is done.
- To prepare using a rice cooker, combine washed and drained rice with cooled dressing and cook until done.

# FRIED RICE WITH CHICKEN AND PRAWNS
## (NASI GORENG)

For a healthier version, use a non-stick pan and reduce the amount of oil used. A one-dish meal, fried rice can be prepared with any combination of meat and vegetables. Use leftover meat liberally.

### Ingredients

| | |
|---|---|
| Vegetable oil | 90 ml (3 fl oz) |
| Shallots | 70 g (2¹/2 oz), peeled, halved lengthways and sliced |
| Garlic | 50 g (2 oz), peeled and sliced |
| Red chillies | 2, large, halved, seeded and finely sliced |
| Bird's eye chillies (optional) | 2, finely sliced |
| Cabbage | 100 g (3¹/2 oz), sliced into strips |
| Spiced tomato sauce (see pg 9) | 1 Tbsp |
| Chicken meat | 150 g (5 oz), diced, preferably dark meat |
| Prawns (shrimps) | 150 g (5 oz), medium, shelled and cleaned |
| Salty soy sauce (kecap asin) | 2 Tbsp |
| Eggs | 2, beaten |
| Cooked rice | 600 g (1 lb 5 oz), chilled |
| Chinese celery leaves | 25 g (1 oz), sliced |
| Leek | 50 g (2 oz), small, sliced |
| Spring onions (scallions) | 50 g (2 oz), sliced |
| Spinach | 50 g (2 oz), sliced |
| Salt | a pinch or to taste |
| Crisp-fried shallots | 2 Tbsp |

Sauté shallots, garlic and chillies until golden yellow before adding cabbage, spiced tomato sauce, chicken and prawns.

Add in eggs and soy sauce when ingredients in pan are well mixed and cabbage has softened slightly.

### Method

- Heat oil in a wok or heavy frying pan (skillet). Add shallots, garlic and chillies. Sauté over medium heat for 1 minute or until golden yellow.
- Add cabbage, spiced tomato sauce, chicken and prawns. Fry again for 1 minute.
- Add soy sauce and eggs. Fry until eggs are scrambled and mixture of ingredients is dry or liquid-free.
- Add rice and fry for 3 minutes, then add all remaining ingredients. Mix well.
- Adjust to taste with more salt if necessary. Dish out and serve.

# RICE PORRIDGE WITH CHICKEN
## (BUBUR AYAM)

This recipe can be prepared with short instead of long grain rice for a risotto dish. Reduce chicken stock to 1 litre (1³/5 pints / 4 cups) and top with more when necessary during cooking process.

### Ingredients

| | |
|---|---|
| Chicken | 1, about 1.2 kg (2 lb 10 oz) |
| Vegetable oil | 2 Tbsp |
| Shallots | 50 g (2 oz), peeled and sliced |
| Garlic | 30 g (1 oz), peeled and sliced |
| *Salam* leaves | 3, left whole |
| Lemon grass | 1 stalk, bruised or shredded and knotted |
| Long grain rice | 300 g (10¹/2 oz), washed, rinsed for 1 minute and drained |
| Chicken stock (see pg 10) | 1.5 litres (2²/5 pints / 6 cups) |
| Salt | to taste |
| Crushed black peppercorns | to taste |
| Crisp-fried shallots | 2 Tbsp |

### Topping

| | |
|---|---|
| Shredded chicken | 800 g (1 lb 5 oz) |
| Chicken spice paste (see pg 8) | 2 Tbsp |
| Vegetable oil | 1 Tbsp |
| Spring onions (scallions) | 50 g (2 oz), sliced |
| Chinese celery leaves | 50 g (2 oz), sliced |
| Bird's eye chillies | 2, chopped |

**Step-By-Step**

Sauté shallots, garlic, *salam* leaves and lemon grass for 2 minutes before adding rice.

After sautéing the rice, add in half the chicken stock prepared earlier and reserved after allowing chicken to cool in it.

If preferred, stir a portion of garnishing ingredients into porridge before dividing into individual serving bowls.

### Method

- Prepare chicken stock. When stock has simmered for 4 hours, add chicken and simmer for 1 hour or until chicken is very tender and meat almost falls off the bone.
- Remove chicken from stock and place inside a deep container. Strain stock through a fine sieve over chicken. Leave chicken to cool in stock.
- Remove chicken from cold stock, separate meat from bones and shred very finely. Set aside.

- Prepare porridge. Heat oil in a heavy saucepan. Add shallots, garlic, *salam* leaves and lemon grass. Sauté for 2 minutes.
- Add rice and sauté for 1 minute.
- Add half the chicken stock, bring to the boil and simmer until rice is very soft but not overcooked. While simmering, top up with more stock as it evaporates.
- Mix in half the shredded chicken. Season to taste with salt and black pepper.

- Combine remaining shredded chicken with all topping ingredients. Mix well. Season to taste with salt and black pepper.
- Divide porridge into 4 serving bowls. Garnish each with 2 rounded (heaped) Tbsp topping.
- Garnish with crisp-fried shallots and serve.

Cook noodles in rapidly boiling water at a ratio of 500 g (1 lb 1 1/2 oz) noodles to 5 litres (8 pints / 20 cups) water.

If not using the noodles immediately, rinse with cold water, then toss with 2 Tbsp vegetable oil to prevent sticking.

After adding noodles, fry for 3 minutes or until ingredients are well mixed before adding remaining ingredients.

S t e p - B y - S t e p

# FRIED NOODLES WITH VEGETABLES
## (*MIE GORENG*)

This dish is similar to the fried rice recipe on page 89 in terms of the meat and vegetable combination, but that can be tweaked to taste. Although egg noodles are used here, the dish can also be prepared with pasta of choice.

### Ingredients

| | |
|---|---|
| Cooked egg noodles | 600 g (1 lb 5 oz), chilled |
| Vegetable oil | 90 ml (3 fl oz) |
| Shallots | 70 g (2 1/2 oz), peeled, halved lengthways and sliced |
| Garlic | 50 g (2 oz), peeled and sliced |
| Red chillies | 2, large, halved, seeded and finely sliced |
| Bird's eye chillies (optional) | 2, finely sliced |
| Cabbage | 100 g (3 1/2 oz), sliced into strips |
| Spiced tomato sauce (see pg 9) | 1 Tbsp |
| Salty soy sauce (*kecap asin*) | 2 Tbsp |
| Eggs | 2, beaten |
| Chinese celery leaves | 40 g (1 1/4 oz), sliced |
| Leek | 60 g (2 oz), small, sliced |
| Spring onions (scallions) | 80 g (2 3/4 oz), sliced |
| Spinach | 80 g (2 3/4 oz), sliced |
| Crisp-fried shallots | 2 Tbsp |
| Salt | a pinch or to taste |

### Method

- The noodles must be cooked in rapidly boiling water at a ratio of 500 g (1 lb 1 1/2 oz) noodles to 5 litres (8 pints / 20 cups) water. Add 1 Tbsp oil and 2 Tbsp salt to the boiling water. The noodles, and all pastas for that matter, must be cooked uncovered and to the *al dente* stage, which literally means "to the tooth". The cooked pasta should be slightly resistant to the bite and have no taste of raw flour.

- Drain noodles just before the *al dente* stage is reached and leave to cool. If not using immediately, rinse with cold water and drain again, then toss with 2 Tbsp vegetable oil, which will prevent sticking.

- Heat vegetable oil in wok or heavy frying pan (skillet). Add shallots, garlic and chillies. Sauté over medium heat for 1 minute or until golden yellow.

- Add cabbage and spiced tomato sauce. Fry again for 1 minute, then add soy sauce and fry until dry.

- Add eggs and continue frying until eggs are scrambled.

- Add noodles and fry for 3 minutes, then add remaining ingredients, mix well and season to taste.

- Dish out and serve garnished with vegetable crackers if desired.

Black Rice Pudding (*Bubuh Injin*)

Coconut Pancake (*Dadar*)

Fried Bananas (*Godoh Biu*)

Green Bean Pudding (*Bubuh Kacang Ijo*)

Iced Fruit in Coconut Dressing (*Es Campur*)

Rice Flour Dumplings in Palm Sugar Syrup (*Jaja Batun Bedil*)

Steamed Jackfruit Cake (*Sumping Nangka*)

Soak the rice for a minimum of 8 hours, if not overnight, before use.

Sufficiently soaked rice is softer and will cook to a consistency similar to risotto.

Lastly, melt palm sugar into glutinous rice and adjust to taste with a pinch of salt. Adding sugar and salt any sooner will cause the rice to cook unevenly.

S t e p - B y - S t e p

# BLACK RICE PUDDING
## (*BUBUH INJIN*)

A classic dessert of black and white glutinous rice, *bubuh injin* is substantial enough to double-up as an afternoon snack.

### Ingredients

| | |
|---|---|
| Black glutinous rice | 250 g (9 oz) |
| White glutinous rice | 75 g (2$^1$/$_2$ oz) |
| Water | 1.25 litres (2 pints / 5 cups) |
| Screwpine (*pandan*) leaf | 1 |
| Palm sugar | 175 g (6 oz) or to taste |
| Salt | a pinch or to taste |
| Coconut cream | 375 ml (12 fl oz / 1$^1$/$_2$ cups) |

### Method

- Rinse black and white glutinous rice well under running water. Soak overnight and drain before using.
- Combine 750 ml water, both types of glutinous rice and screwpine leaf in a heavy pan. Simmer over medium heat for about 45 minutes, adding more water if necessary.
- Add palm sugar and continue to cook until most liquid has evaporated. Season to taste with salt. Remove from heat and leave to cool.
- Serve at room temperature topped with desired amounts of coconut cream.

# COCONUT PANCAKES
## (*DADAR*)

Coconut pancakes are like soft, sweet spring rolls when served. They can be served as an after-meal dessert or a tea-time snack.

### Ingredients

| | |
|---|---|
| Rice flour | 100 g (3$\frac{1}{2}$ oz) |
| Sugar | 30 g (1 oz) |
| Salt | a pinch |
| Eggs | 3 |
| Coconut milk | 250 ml (8 fl oz / 1 cup) |
| Vegetable oil | 2 Tbsp |

### Palm Sugar Syrup

| | |
|---|---|
| Palm sugar | 375 g (12$\frac{1}{2}$ oz), chopped |
| Water | 250 ml (8 fl oz / 1 cup) |

### Coconut Filling

| | |
|---|---|
| Palm sugar syrup | 125 ml (4 fl oz / $\frac{1}{2}$ cup) |
| Grated coconut | 125 g (4$\frac{1}{2}$ oz) |
| Screwpine (*pandan*) leaf | 1, bruised |

Step-By-Step

Pour in 1 ladleful or about 4 Tbsp batter into a heated non-stick pan to make a thin pancake. Turn over when batter has set.

Add grated coconut to reheated palm sugar syrup and cook for 2 minutes, mixing until well coated and evenly coloured.

To prepare pancake rolls, spoon 1 Tbsp coconut filling along the centre of the pancake, then fold in left and right sides and roll up.

### Method

- Prepare pancakes. Combine all ingredients in a large bowl and mix well. Stir well with a balloon whisk until lump-free, then strain. Batter should be very liquid in consistency.
- Heat a non-stick pan over low heat. Add 4 Tbsp batter to form a very thin pancake.
- Turn over when batter has set. Repeat until mixture is used up. Leave pancakes to cool to room temperature.
- Prepare palm sugar syrup. Combine palm sugar and water in a saucepan and bring to the boil. Simmer for 10 minutes, then remove from heat and leave to cool before using.
- Prepare coconut filling. Heat palm sugar syrup in a frying pan (skillet). Add grated coconut and screwpine leaf and mix well. Cook over low heat for 2 minutes.
- Place 1 Tbsp filling along the centre of a pancake. Fold in left and right sides, then roll up.

# FRIED BANANAS
## (*GODOH BIU*)

Sweet and fragrant bananas with crispy outer coatings, *godoh biu* has been unfailingly popular with the whole family. It also could not be easier to prepare.

### Ingredients

| | |
|---|---|
| Rice flour | 100 g (3½ oz) |
| Plain (all-purpose) flour | 50 g (2 oz) |
| Water | 160 ml (5½ oz) |
| Salt | a pinch |
| Finger bananas | 8, peeled and halved lengthways, or 4 large bananas, peeled and sliced |

Cooking oil for deep-frying

Step-By-Step

Make sure banana pieces are well coated with batter before lowering into hot oil to cook.

A variation of the fried banana recipe involves mashing the bananas first, then mixing in flour, water, sugar and a pinch of salt. See method below for quantities.

Lower in tablespoonfuls of mashed banana batter into hot oil to cook until crisp and golden brown in colour.

### Method

- Combine both types of flour, water and salt in a mixing bowl. Whisk until batter is smooth and slightly thick.
- Dip banana slices into batter and coat generously.
- Heat oil for deep-frying to 160°C/325°F. Place battered bananas into hot oil one at a time to prevent them from sticking.

- Deep-fry over low heat until battered bananas are golden brown and very crispy.
- Drain well on absorbent paper towels. Serve with palm sugar syrup (see pg 99).
- For a variation known as *jaja pulung biu*, mash 400 g (13½ oz) very ripe bananas, then add 100 g (3½ oz) plain

(all-purpose) flour, 160 ml (5½ oz) water, 30 g (1 oz) sugar and a pinch of salt and mix until a soft elastic dough results. Deep-fry tablespoonfuls of dough in 160°C/325°F oil until crisp and golden, then drain on absorbent paper and serve with palm sugar syrup.

Although dry-frying the beans is not absolutely necessary, taking the time to do it adds a pleasant roasted aroma to the dessert.

With beans in a pot, add water and ginger, then bring to the boil and simmer until beans are almost cooked.

Add coconut milk, sugar, salt and screwpine leaf, if used, when beans are nearly cooked. Simmer for 10 minutes more.

Step-By-Step

# GREEN BEAN PUDDING
## (*BUBUH KACANG IJO*)

The Balinese enjoy eating this dessert with a generous helping of condensed milk poured over the top.

### Ingredients

| | |
|---|---|
| Green (mung) beans | 340 g (11$^1$/$_2$ oz) |
| Water | 1.5 litres (2$^2$/$_5$ pints / 6 cups) |
| Ginger | 50 g (2 oz), peeled, sliced and crushed |
| Coconut milk | 500 ml (16 fl oz / 2 cups) |
| Sugar | 125 g (4$^1$/$_2$ oz) |
| Salt | a pinch |
| Screwpine (*pandan*) leaf (optional) | 1, washed and knotted |

### Method

- Clean green beans thoroughly under running water, removing all loose skins and impurities.
- If preferred, enhance the flavour of the green beans by dry-frying them briefly in a heavy pan over medium heat. This will add a slightly roasted flavour, but be careful not to burn them.

- Combine green beans, water and ginger in a heavy pot. Bring to the boil and simmer for about 30 minutes or until beans are about 80 per cent cooked. Top with more water if required.
- Add all remaining ingredients and simmer for 10 minutes. Remove from heat and leave to cool to room temperature.

- Serve topped with grated coconut or coconut cream if desired. Alternatively, refrigerate after leaving to cool and serve with some ice cubes or shaved ice.

Peel and dice sweet potatoes and fruit of choice. The top left bowl shows what ingredients should look like after boiling in palm sugar syrup.

Boil sweet potato pieces and palm fruits until they are almost soft before adding fruit pieces, which take much less time to cook.

Mix in coconut cream towards the end of the cooking process and finish with lime juice before removing from heat.

# ICED FRUIT IN COCONUT DRESSING
## (*ES CAMPUR*)

An exciting mix of tropical fruits with a creamy coconut dressing that is sweetened by palm sugar and brushed with subtle screwpine fragrance.

### *Ingredients*

| | |
|---|---|
| Rice flour dumplings (see pg 107) | 200 g (7 oz) |
| Palm sugar | 375 g (12$^1$/$_2$ oz), chopped |
| Water | 250 ml (8 fl oz / 1 cup) |
| Screwpine (*pandan*) leaf | 1, bruised |
| Sweet potatoes | 200 g (7 oz), peeled and diced |
| Palm fruit | 200 g (7 oz) |
| Diced mixed fruit of choice | 200 g (7 oz), use pineapple, mango, jackfruit and/or bananas |
| Coconut cream | 50 ml (1$^3$/4 oz) |
| Lime juice | 2 Tbsp |

### *Method*

- Prepare rice flour dumplings and set aside.
- Bring palm sugar, water and screwpine leaf to the boil and simmer for 5 minutes.

- Add sweet potatoes and palm fruit. Simmer until almost soft.
- Add mixed fruit and dumplings. Return to the boil and simmer for 2 minutes.
- Mix in coconut cream, return to the boil and simmer 1 minute more.

- Finish by adding lime juice, then remove from heat and leave to cool.
- Serve at room temperature or chilled and topped with ice.

# RICE FLOUR DUMPLINGS IN PALM SUGAR SAUCE
## (JAJA BATUN BEDIL)

A dessert of rice flour dumplings bathed in a rich palm sugar syrup.

### Ingredients

| | |
|---|---|
| Glutinous rice flour | 150 g (5 oz) |
| Tapioca (cassava) flour | 60 g (2 oz) |
| Salt | a pinch |
| Water | 180 ml (6 fl oz / $1/2$ cup) |

### Sauce

| | |
|---|---|
| Water | 125 ml (4 fl oz / $1/2$ cup) |
| Coconut milk | 125 ml (4 fl oz / $1/2$ cup) |
| Palm sugar | 125 g ($4^{1}/2$ oz), chopped |
| Screwpine (pandan) leaf | 1, bruised |
| Salt | a pinch |

S t e p - B y - S t e p

The resulting dough should be soft, elastic and not dry. Shape into 1-cm ($1/2$-inch) dumplings.

Cook dumplings in plenty of lightly salted water. When the balls float to the surface, they are cooked.

Lower cooled dumplings into palm sugar syrup and simmer for 20 minutes or until brown from absorbing syrup.

### Method

- Prepare dumplings. Combine both flours and salt in a bowl. Gradually mix in water and knead until a smooth dough results. The dough should be soft, elastic and not dry.
- Shape dough into dumplings about 1-cm ($1/2$-inch) in diameter.
- Bring 4 litres ($6^{2}/5$ pints / 16 cups) of lightly salted water to the boil.
- Add dumplings, return to the boil and simmer for 5 minutes.
- Drain dumplings and lower into ice water to cool.
- Prepare sauce. Combine all ingredients in a saucepan, bring to the boil and simmer for 5 minutes.
- Add dumplings and simmer for 20 minutes over very low heat.
- Remove from heat and leave to cool to room temperature.
- Serve with freshly grated coconut and coconut cream if desired.

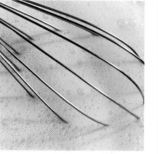

Use a balloon whisk to mix rice flour, sugar, coconut milk and salt together. The resulting mixture should be lump-free.

When over heat, mixture should be stirred continuously until thickened and lump-free.

To wrap, first fold banana leaf in thirds, then fold down left and right ends so weight of parcel rests on them to secure.

**S t e p - B y - S t e p**

# STEAMED JACKFRUIT CAKE
## (*SUMPING NANGKA*)

The unique taste of jackfruit is balanced by the mild fragrance of banana leaf and robust flavour of coconut milk in this pleasant and light dessert.

### Ingredients

| | |
|---|---|
| Rice flour | 180 g (6 oz) |
| Sugar | 80 g (2 3/4 oz) |
| Coconut milk | 500 ml (16 fl oz / 2 cups) |
| Salt | a pinch |
| Banana leaf squares | 12, each 15 x 15 cm (6 x 6 inches) |
| Jackfruit segments | 12, halved |

### Method

- Combine rice flour, sugar, coconut milk and salt in a large bowl. Mix well and until lump-free.
- Slowly bring mixture to the boil in a non-stick pan. Simmer until mixture thickens, stirring continuously until smooth and lump-free. Remove from heat and leave to cool.

- Place 1 rounded (heaped) Tbsp cooked mixture onto a banana leaf square. Top with a slice of jackfruit and cover with 1 Tbsp mixture.
- Fold banana leaf in thirds lengthways, then fold down left and right ends so the weight of the parcel rests on them. Repeat until ingredients are used up.

- Steam parcels for about 20 minutes or until cooked. Remove and leave to cool.
- Serve at room temperature.

Glossary of Ingredients

Index

# GLOSSARY OF INGREDIENTS

**Candlenuts**

Known as *tingkih* in Bali and *kemiri* in Indonesia, candlenuts (*below*) are yellowish, brittle and waxy. They are used mainly as a binding agent but also impart a faint flavour to the dish. If unavailable, use shelled and skinned raw peanuts.

**Chillies**

The Balinese love chillies (*below*) in their food and often use an amount that is far beyond the taste of most Westerners. Three main types—large, small and bird's eye—are used in Balinese cooking. Large chillies (pictured), or *tabia lombok* to the Balinese, are the mildest of the three, with nearly no bite at all, and they are mostly added to a dish for flavouring rather than bite.

Small chillies, or *tabia Bali*, grow to an average length of 2.5 cm (1 inch) and are the most commonly used on the island. Usually chopped or bruised, small chillies give a great kick.

Bird's eye chillies, or *tabia kerinyi*, are the smallest and also the most potent in terms of fiery hotness. They are usually served raw and as a condiment.

**Black glutinous rice**

The Balinese most often use black glutinous rice (*top*) to make cakes or snacks. Probably the most common preparation is black rice pudding, which is served with palm sugar and coconut cream. The black rice grains are short, stubby and only black on the outside. They are white at the centre. However, because the black colouring is water soluble, it is able to penetrate the rice grain with cooking. Black glutinous rice is also considerablely more expensive than its white counterpart. In the fields, black glutinous rice looks much like ordinary rice, and the grains on the stalks are not black.

**Blimbing**

Known to Malay speakers as *belimbing*, these thumb-sized fruit impart a zesty, tangy flavour to the dish. Blimbing (*above*) are sometimes referred to as sour star fruit because they belong to the same botanical family of carambola.

### Coconut

Freshly grated coconut (*below*), or *nyuh*, is perhaps the most used ingredient in Balinese cooking. Many vegetable and meat dishes, as well as most cakes use coconut as flavouring.

Another important use of coconut is to provide coconut milk, which is, in turn, the source of coconut oil. In order to make coconut milk, and later oil, one must first dehusk the coconut in order to expose the inner nut. This is mostly done by hand and requires not only strength, but also know-how. The inner nut is then broken with a rock or hammer or by throwing it against a hard surface. The meat can then be taken out with the help of a flat tool which is inserted between the shell and the meat. Once removed, the brown outer skin is peeled off and the remaining coconut shredded finely.

In many Western countries, freshly shredded coconut is now available vacuum-packed in Asian and regular supermarkets. If freshly grated coconut is unavailable, desiccated coconut moistened with coconut milk can be used as a substitute.

### Coriander seeds

Balinese cooks use dried coriander seeds (*above*), or *ketumbah*, in many dishes. The seeds are thoroughly crushed before use. The seeds used in Bali are no different from the ones found in the West.

### Galangal

Also known as "blue ginger", galangal (*above*) is known to the Balinese as *isen*, and to the Indonesians as *laos*. The rhizome is sold fresh, dried or ground. Today, it is readily available fresh in Asian shops and supermarkets in the West.

### Dried prawn (shrimp) paste

*Trasi* or *terasi* to the Balinese, the brown, pungent paste is made by pounding sun-dried prawns to a pulp. Dried prawn paste (*below*) must be grilled or roasted in a dry pan before use. This neutralises the strong, fishy flavour. Once roasted, the paste can be stored for several months in an airtight container, preferably glass jar. Although pungent, and sometimes unpleasantly so, before cooking, dried prawn paste adds incredible flavour to the dish.

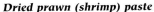

### Garlic

The garlic, or *kesuna*, found in Bali (*below*) is similar to Western garlic, except that the cloves are usually much smaller and the flavour is also slightly less pungent. Indonesians generally know garlic as *bawang putih*.

### Kaffir limes

Kaffir limes (*left*), or *juuk purut* to the Balinese, are small and have very knobby skin. The Balinese often use small quantities to spice up certain dishes. If unavailable, however, the common lime is an acceptable substitute.

Kaffir lime leaves are also used, usually whole in soups or sauces and finely chopped for fish, chicken and duck dishes.

### Ginger

Known to the Balinese as *jahe*, ginger (*left*) was one of the earliest spices imported from the native jungles of Southeast Asia. The underground rhizome of an attractive flowering plant, ginger is widely used in Balinese cooking. The rhizome should be plump and firm, and must always be peeled before use. After peeling, either slice or pound the flesh. Fresh ginger is readily available in most Asian stores, and ground or powdered ginger should never be used as a substitute.

### Lemon basil

Different kinds of basil, varying greatly in flavour and aroma, grow throughout Asia. Native to tropical Asia, where it has been cultivated for the past 3,000 years, lemon basil (*above*) is now grown wherever the climate is warm. Known to Indonesians as *don kemangi*, lemon basil is a delicate herb with a pleasant flavour, which is as its name suggests a combination of lemon and basil. In Bali, lemon basil is most commonly used in soups, salads and fish dishes, especially those involving banana leaf wrappers.

### Lemon grass

Lemon grass (*below*), or *sere* to the Balinese, is used in many Balinese dishes. Lemon grass stalks must be peeled and bruised to release their fragrance before use. Alternatively, they have to be finely sliced because the stalks are extremely fibrous. When used in a spice paste or sauce, bruise the lemon grass stalk along its entire length, then tie into a knot. This will prevent the fibres from separating and spreading throughout the dish. If unavailable, substitute with lemon or lime zest.

### Nutmeg

The nutmeg (*above*), or *jebug garum*, is the hard kernel of the fruit of an evergreen tree native to the Moluccas of the Spice Islands. Avoid using ground or powdered nutmeg as much of its pungency would have been lost. Always grate whole nutmeg to use. This aromatic and sweet spice is usually used with strongly flavoured meats such as pork, duck and lamb.

### Peanuts (Groundnuts)

Always look for raw peanuts with the skins still on (*below*). This is because when the peanuts have been deep-fried or roasted until golden brown, the skins become intensely flavourful and can enhance the flavour of a dish by up to 75 per cent. If unavailable, substitute with peanuts that have been roasted in their shells.

### Peppercorns

The Balinese use black pepper (*above*) much more frequently than white pepper in their cooking. The peppercorns are always freshly ground or crushed until fine just before using. Ready ground pepper is rarely used because much of its aroma has already been lost.

### Salam leaves

*Salam* leaves (*below*) are used in much the same way bay leaves are used, and the two also appear quite similar. As a result, *salam* leaves are often mislabelled Indonesian bay leaves by suppliers. In fact, *salam* leaves belong to the myrtle family, which is unrelated to the laurel family of bay leaves. If unavailable, just omit ingredient from recipe; do not use a substitute. Its flavour, while mild, is inimitable.

### Screwpine (pandan) leaves

Better known as *pandan* leaves, screwpine leaves (*above*) are aromatic and mostly used for flavouring cakes and snacks. In Bali, screwpine leaves are often shredded to put on top of offering baskets meant for the gods.

### Shallots

The common onion of Bali, shallots (*left*), or *bawang merah*, are small and red. They are similar but not identical to shallots sold in other parts of the world. If unavailable, substitute with the same amount of red Spanish onions.

116

### Soy sauce

Two main types of soy sauce are used in Indonesian, and correspondingly Balinese, cooking. Indonesian salty soy sauce (*kecap asin*) (*bottom, left*) is similar enough but, nevertheless, different from Chinese or Japanese soy sauces. Indonesian sweet soy sauce (*kecap manis*) (*bottom, right*) is considerably tastier than its salty counterpart. Today, the ABC brand of soy sauce is available in just about every Asian shop the world over.

### Turmeric

Also known as "yellow ginger", turmeric (*above*) is an attractive perennial plant with large, lily-like leaves and yellow flowers. Its brownish skin must be scraped away to expose the bright yellow-orange flesh below before use. If fresh turmeric is unavailable, use 1 Tbsp ground or powdered turmeric for every 100 g (3$^1$/$_2$ oz) fresh turmeric called for in a recipe.

For turmeric water, combine 1 cup finely chopped turmeric with 250 ml (8 fl oz / 1 cup) water in a blender (processor) and blend until fine. In Bali, fresh turmerc is pounded in a stone mortar until very fine and then mixed with water. The mixture is left to rest for 5 minutes before it is strained through a fine sieve. It is customary to press down firmly on the pulp to extract all the juice possible.

### Tamarind

Tamarind pulp, which the Balinese know as *celagi* or *lunak*, is derived from large, dark brown pods (*below*) that grow from the tamarind tree. The fleshy pulp is sour-tasting and contains a lot of hard seeds. To use tamarind pulp, mix it with some warm water and let it stand for 15 minutes, then strain using a fine strainer for tamarind juice to add to the dish.

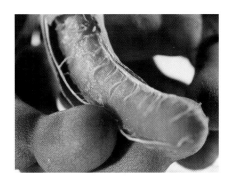

# INDEX